Albatros D.Va

D.5390/17

A Pictorial History and Description of the Famous German WWI Fighter

Colin A. Owers

Albatros D.Va

D.5390/17

A Pictorial History and Description of the Famous German WWI Fighter

Colin A. Owers

Great War Aviation Centennial Series #90

Acknowledgements

Color aircraft profiles © Bob Pearson. While every care is taken, some colors are speculative based on known practices at the time. Purchase Bob's CD of WWI aircraft profiles for $50 US/Canadian, 40 €, or £30, airmail postage included, via Paypal to Bob.

For information on our aviation books, please see our website at: **www.aeronautbooks.com**. Aeronaut Books is looking for photographs of rare German aircraft of WWI for our books. To help please contact the publisher at **jherris@me.com**.

Interested in WWI aviation? Join The League of WWI Aviation Historians (**www.overthefront.com**), Cross & Cockade International (**www.crossandcockade.com**), and Das Propellerblatt (**www.propellerblatt.de**).

ISBN: 978-1-964637-06-8

Cover Painting: *The Duellists* by Steven Hayen
   hppts://stevenheyenart.com
Design and layout: Jack Herris
Cover design: Aaron Weaver
Color Profiles: Bob Pearson; bpearson@kaien.net
Digital photo editing: Jack Herris

Aeronaut Books

Books for Enthusiasts by Enthusiasts
www.aeronautbooks.com

Table of Contents

Introduction   4

Chapter 1: Development of the Albatros D.Va   5

Chapter 2: No. 3 Squadron, AFC   11

Chapter 3: The Duellists   13

Chapter 4: Albatros D.5390/17 in Australia   24

Chapter 5: The Wings   41

Chapter 6: The Aerofoil Radiator   56

Chapter 7: The Fuselage   64

Chapter 8: Engine, Propeller, and Armament   79

Chapter 9: The Cockpit   85

Chapter 10: The Tailplane, Fin, and Rudder   92

Chapter 11: The Undercarriage   98

Chapter 12: Colours and Markings   108

Afterword: What British Pilots Thought of the Albatros D.Va   116

Drawings   117

Bibliography   120

R.E.8 A3816
Lt. JLM Sandy / Sgt. HF Hughes
No. 3 Sqdn AFC
December 1917
Reconstruction from available data

Introduction

I had been involved with the restoration and conservation of the Albatros D.Va and Pfalz D.XII scouts of the Australian War Memorial's (AWM) collection from when the Albatros was taken to Camden airfield, NSW, in 1966 for its first restoration since it was brought to Australia following WWI. Up to this time the AWM had only repaired the machines as needed. As will be seen from the photographs the Albatros really needed a through restoration.

I will be the first to admit that these aircraft needed the restoration work done by skilled conservators, and not by enthusiastic amateurs without any overall supervision.

Over the years I obtained many photographs of D.5390/17 as well as material on Albatros aircraft. Much was from friends, by exchanges or by purchases, and I have been fortunate in having some WWI aviation collections given to me. William 'Bill' Toohey gave me his entire collection of photographs and books. The late Alan Fraser left me his collection of notes, articles, etc., relating to the Australian Flying Corps in WWI. I corresponded with the late Bob Waugh for many years. Bob spent years trying to develop a full set of detailed drawings of the Albatros and Pfalz fighters. Bob's work was so good that the Smithsonian National Air and Space Museum (NASM) used his notes in the restoration, actually, more a rebuild, of their Albatros D.Va. Bob's plans of the D.Va grace the pages of the NASM's book on the restoration – *Albatros D.Va German Fighter of World War I*. (Smithsonian Institute Press, USA. 1980). Every letter I received from Bob would contain a sketch where he was struggling to make the information that he was receiving from around the world, fit into his final set of plans. He wrote to me saying he was leaving me a set of his final plans, however this never eventuated.

While working at Demondrille Shire, Harden, NSW, I used to come to the Australian Society for Aero Historical Preservation Ltd weekends working on the AWM's Pfalz D.XII and de Havilland D.H.9 aircraft in the shed at the Royal Military College, Duntroon, Canberra, where they had been stored. Later, I was residing at Boorowa, NSW, and volunteered at the AWM where I wrote captions for their WWI aviation photographs. When I retired to Canberra, I reapplied to the AWM and have been working in the Military Heraldry and Technology section for a number of years. This has given me the opportunity to photograph the aircraft of the AWM.

It seemed a waste to have this information and not to publish it so that historians, modellers and enthusiasts could have access to it.

This work came from a tentative question on the ADF Serials Military Group Facebook page as to whether such a book would be welcome.

I have had a lot of help over the years and made many friends, too many of which are no longer with us. Acknowledgement is due to:
The late Jack Bruce; Shane Casey; Peter Chapman; Mark Clayton; Nick Fletcher; the late Peter M. Grosz; Trevor Henshaw; Jack Herris; the late Neville Hewitt; Colin Huston; Sir Peter Jackson; Laura Kennedy; Ray Rimell; the late Bruce Robertson; the late Charles 'Chaz' Schaedel; William 'Bill' Toohey; Greg van Wyngarden; the late Eric Watson; the late Bob Waugh; and John White.

Any errors are mine alone.

Above: Typical letter from Bob Waugh with his sketches of the Albatros D.Va.

Glossary

AFC	Australian Flying Corps
AWM	Australian War Museum/Australian War Memorial
Capt	Captain
HMT	His Majesty's Transport
Lt	Lieutenant
NSW	New South Wales
RAF	Royal Air Force
RFC	Royal Flying Corps
Sergt	Sergeant

Development of the Albatros D.Va

Prinz Friedrich Karl von Preußen in seinem selbstkonstruierten Kampfflugzeug, mit dem er abstürzte und schwerverwundet in Gefangenschaft geriet.

Zensiert
Paul Hoffmann & Co.
Berlin-Schöneberg.

Above: Prince Friedrich Karl of Prussia in his Albatros D.I. The height of the upper wing above the cockpit can be clearly seen as can the box-type side radiators. On a patrol with *Jasta* 2 on 12 March 1917, his aircraft was brought down by a bullet in his engine. He was also wounded in the foot. Making a successful force landing in no-man's land, he was running towards his own lines when he was shot in the back by Australian troops. He was taken into captivity where he passed away, due to his wounds, on 6 April 1917, his 24th birthday.

When WWI broke out in August 1914, very few leaders of the armies involved had any idea of air power. The aircraft of 1914 were used for reconnaissance, but once the conflict developed into trench warfare, it begam an artillery duel, each side hoping to open the enemy's lines to allow for their troop and cavalry to break through and end the war.[1]

From pre-war days, visionaries in many countries saw that control of the sky was necessary and this would be achieved by armed aircraft. Many of the personnel involved also looked to arm their aircraft because they wanted to 'get at' their opponents. Various schemes were devised to install armament onto aircraft, some bizarre and others effective for their time. The tractor aircraft had the problem of the airscrew in front leading to machine-guns being installed on the upper wing where they fired over the airscrew's arc, such as the Nieuport 11.

The ideal machine at the time appeared to be the pusher where the engine was mounted behind the crew giving the gunner a clear field of fire forward. The Vickers E.F.B.1 was displayed at the 1913 Olympia Aero Show. It was a two-seat pusher with the tail surfaces mounted on twin booms. *The Aeroplane* reported that *Contrary to the usual custom, the passenger, armed with a new type quick-firer, is perched out in front of everything where he has an uninterrupted range of view and weapon.*[2] This layout was basically the same for all the pusher fighters, two-seat or single-seat, that followed.

The Vickers 'Gun Bus' was to be successful on the Western Front for a short time, but it could not hold its own against the Fokker Eindecker with an interrupter gear that allowed it to fire a machine gun through the airscrew arc. The story of Anthony Fokker and his development of the single-seat fighter has been told many times and need nor repeating here except to say that the single-seat fighter continues to be the mainstay of fighter forces to this day.

Above: The lowered upper wing of the Albatros D.II is well shown here, together with the N type cabane struts. Note also the airfoil radiator mounted in the center section of the upper wing. This particular example was taken by the French and tested in French markings although they kept the serial number 910.

Fighter aircraft were developed to protect the reconnaissance and artillery aircraft that photographed the lines and directed the artillery in counter battery work. Control of the air was now the object of both sides. This led to the development of fighter aircraft in speed, range, and firepower. Control swung back and forth between the Allies and the Central Powers.

The Fokker Eindecker monoplanes were not good fighting aircraft and were followed by biplanes designed from the start as fighters. Early Halberstadt and Fokker fighters were unable to wrest control of the air from the British de Havilland D.H.2 pusher and Nieuport 11 fighters. In August 1916 Albatros Werke of Johannisthal, Berlin, brought out its D.I biplane fighter powered by a 160-hp Mercedes engine, and carrying twin Maxim 08/15 synchronised machine guns. The wings were of conventional construction around two spars and fabric covered. The fuselage was a frame of longerons and formers that was covered with plywood. A large spinner completed the rakish fuselage.

There was only one criticism of the D.I by the military authorities, and that was that the upper wing obscured the pilot's view in the forward and upward direction. The company brought the wing closer to the fuselage in their D.II and replaced the trestle-type cabane struts of the D.I with splayed N-type struts. Late D.II fighters also had aerofoil radiators in their upper wing replacing the box like radiators fixed on each side of the fuselage of the D.I and early D.II fighters.

The D.I and D.II obtained ascendency for the German *Jastas*, the Albatros proving superior to its Allied opponents.

The D.II was followed by the D.III that arrived at the front in January 1917. In order to improve downward visibility, the Albatros engineers had adopted a the 'vee' strut layout of the French Nieuport fighters. Powered by a high-compression version of the 160-hp Mercedes engine, the early models had an aerofoil radiator in the centre of the top wing. This was offset starboard on later models. The German Albatros 'vee strutters', as they were called by their RFC opponents, suffered wing failures. The single spar of the lower wing was positioned too far aft and allowed the wing to twist under stress. The Albatros fighters had inherited the structural weakness of the Nieuport design.

The Austro-Hungarian air service used Albatros fighters built by the Oeffag company.[3] They were to overcome the problems with the lower wing and their D.III continued in production until 1918. Unfortunately, the German built Albatros fighters continued to have problems.

By May 1917, new Allied fighters such as the Spad S.7 and Sopwith Triplane, followed shortly after by the Sopwith Camel and the R.A.F. S.E.5a, were appearing and were better than the D.III. The D.V was built to be a lighter version of the D.III. Powered by a 180-hp Mercedes engine, it was distinguished from the slab-sided D.III by its oval fuselage cross section. The aileron control cables ran through the upper wing. The D.V proved to be little better than the D.III and suffered similar wing failures. The design was

Above: D.III D.2096/16 in French markings after its capture. The pilot, *Ltn* Friedrich-Wilhelm Wichard was from *Jasta* 24 and was forced down on 21 April 1917. The personal insignia has been retained on the fuselage. Note how the Albatros logo on the rudder has not been painted over when French rudder stripes were applied. This machine was sent to the USA for exhibition, ending up at McCook Field with the serial P-13. It was exhibited in New York in January 1919.

Above: Albatros D.636/17 in partial British markings after its capture in the Middle East.

modified in a hurry to produce the D.Va. In addition to being heavier than the D.V, the D.III type aileron control was adopted.

The type continued in service up to the Armistice. By November 1918 the Fokker D.VII was the principal German fighter, and, despite building several experimental prototypes, Albatros never regained its ascendency as a builder of fighter aircraft.

Endnotes

1 For an overview of the development of fighter aircraft see Herris, J. *Genesis of Fighter Aviation in WWI,* Aeronaut Books, USA, 2016.
2 The Olympia Aero-Show.' *The Aeroplane*, 20 February 1913. P.228.
3 See Schiemer, P. *Die Albatros (Oeffag) Jagdflugzeuge der k.u.k. Luftfahrtruppen,* H weishaupt Verlag, Graz, 1984, for the story of these Albatros fighters.

Left & Below Left: The experimental Albatros D.IV used an experimental specially geared 160-hp Mercedes engine, that was buried in the fuselage. It had wings similar to the first Albatros D types while its fuselage resembled that of the D.Va. Engine vibration caused by the reduction gearing was the main problem. It was never armed and remained a single prototype.

Above: Moving an D.V on a German airfield. This machine has the late crosses on a dark colour scheme. It is likely the D.V of Kurt Schönfelder of *Jasta* 7. Fuselage was black with a golden yellow six-pointed star. Schönfelder was *Ltn.d.Res.* Josef Jacobs' wingman.

Above & Below: Albatros D.V D.1162/17 of *Ltn* Ernst Clausnitzer, *Jasta* 4 is shown after capture by the British. Clausnitzer was bought down by Spads of No. 23 Squadron on 16 July 1917, at Poperinghe. The aileron control that passed through the upper wing is well shown. This machine was flown by the British as G.56 and much photographed. Capt Clive Collett was flying it from Turnhouse when the exhaust manifold came loose and is thought to have struck the pilot in the head causing him to lose control. The aircraft spun into the Firth of Forth inverted and Collett drowned.

Above: Albatros D.Va D.5359/17 with other German aircraft abandoned by the Germans at El Afuleh airfield in the Middle East according to one album that they appear in. D.F.W C.V 4432/18 two-seater is in the background. The Germans provided their best aircraft to the Middle East, unlike the British who treated it as a backwater and sent obsolescent aircraft until the final months of 1918.

Above: This photograph of Albatros D.Va D.7416/17 was taken at the same airfield. Note the twin radiators in the upper wing for the desert climate. The Albatros logo is displayed on the rudder. This is reported to be the aircraft of *Fliegerabteilung* 304b leader *Hptm*. Franz Walz, *Pour le Mérite* ace.

No.3 Squadron, AFC

No. 69 Squadron, RFC, better known as No. 3 Squadron, AFC, was a corps reconnaissance squadron engaged on spotting for artillery with a side line of dropping bombs and strafing enemy troop positions. When the Squadron arrived at Bailleul, France, in November 1917, all five Australian Divisions had been brought together on the Somme front as one Corps and this was the Corps that No. 3 Squadron worked with until the Armistice.

The Squadron recorded in their War Diary[1] that from 12 to 15 December 1917, little flying was undertaken due to the consistently bad weather that brought the first snow of the winter. The 15th was fine and much aerial activity occurred from both sides, enemy scouts attempting to interfere with their two-seaters engaged on artillery work. *Several indecisive combats took place.*

On 17 December 1917, it had 16 serviceable and two unserviceable aircraft on charge. During a fine spell in the afternoon R.E.8 No. A3816, aircraft "B", left the ground. Lt James L. Sandy and Sgt Henry F. Hughes were on an *Art. Obs. with 151 SB.8" How Pilot.*[2] That is, they were observing the fall of shot for an 8-inch howitzer battery. *Commenced shoot and carried on till 2.52 p.m. At this time was attacked by 5 E.A. Lt Jones in RE8 A3817 went to his assistance and after indecisive combat EA withdrew. Lt Jones returned for more ammunition leaving Lt Sandy apparently all right. On returning to line Lt Sandy was not seen. Machine not returned nor any reports received at 6.00 pm.*[3]

R.E.8 No. A3817, with a crew of Lt Ern J. Jones and Lt Keith C. Hodgson, had left at 2:00 pm on a Flash Reconnaissance mission, when, at 2:50 pm they saw *5 EA attacking RE8 No. A3816 over DEULEMENT. Went to his assistance and joined in combat. Obs. Fired 400 rounds and at 3.05 pm. EA withdrew. Returned to aerodrome for more ammunition. E.A. had black fuselages with white markings. Under side of wings and tail plane painted light blue.*

Jones flew close to the other R.E.8 to identify it and saw by its number that it was Lt Sandy's machine and appeared to be under control.

Lt H.N. Wrigley with Lt J.R. Blair were also engaged on a *Flash Reconn* in R.E.8 No. B5081. They left at 2.45 p.m. and arrived back at 3.50 p.m. At 3.15 p.m. They observed *5 E.A. S of DEULEMENT engaged by our scouts.* After dropping two 20-lb bombs that both exploded, and the observer firing 100 rounds into enemy trenches, they returned home.[4] According to Wrigley he came upon the scene and *to the crews of both of these aircraft, Lieutenant Sandy's aircraft and crew appeared to be all right…and lieutenant Wrigley proceeded to carry out an artillery reconnaissance.*[5] Wrigley's involvement in the incident is not recorded in the War Diary.

It was not till the following night that word was heard of the machine and then a wire from No. 12 Stationary Hospital, ST. POL, was received, saying that the dead bodies of Lieut. SANDY

and Sergt. HUGHES had been found in a crashed RE8 in a field 5 kilometres N.E of St Pol, near the main Bruay-St. Pol Road.[6]

The Albatros glided to forced landing in front of 21st Battalion's dugouts. The pilot, *Ltn* Rudolf Clauss[8], was wounded in the upper leg.

The German fighter was recovered after dark by a party led by No. 3 Squadron's Engineering Officer, Lt Roderick Ross. The first enemy aircraft brought down intact by AFC.

Sandy had come down in a field 5 kilometres to southeast of St Pol, near the main Bruay-St Pol Rd. Ross believed the machine had flown for two hours before running out of fuel and gliding to a landing. He wrote that *Sgt Hughes was found frozen stiff on the bottom plane apparently having recovered a short period to consciousness and strength to climb but probably with the idea of going for help.*[9]

From a post-mortem of the bodies and an examination of the crash by Capt R. Ross A.F.C. No. 69 Squadron, it would appear that both pilot and observer were killed during the aerial combat; an armoured-piercing bullet having passed through the observer's left lung and then into the base of the pilot's skull. It would appear that the machine had flown itself in left-hand circles until the petrol had exhausted. The direction of the wind of that day being N.W., the machine would drift to the spot where she crashed. There were o witnesses of the crash, and it not found until approximately 20 hours after the occurrence. The ground showed that the machine had come down in a very steep glide, and after hitting one prop blade the right wing touched the ground, and the wind catching the tail, threw the fuselage round in the opposite direction to that in which it hit. Neither Pilot nor Observer was further injured.

The machine was a *Total wreck except for L.H. Wing. Engine Airshaft slightly bent and carburettors and hot air muffs broken. Machine had been salved by No. 16 Squadron RFC.*

Pilot and observer were taken to No. 18 Stationary Hospital.[10]

As *This is the first enemy aeroplane to be brought down by the Australian Flying Corps and the story of the serial battle that brough about this and creates a unique Australian interest in the capture* special representations were made for the machine to be handed over to the Australian authorities for despatch to Australia.[11]

Endnotes:

1 The AFC Squadron War Diaries are available on line on the AWM website. https://www.awm.gov.au/collection/C1338639

2 Both have (P) next to their names, incorrectly indicating that both were pilots. They were observing for the 151st Siege Battery, Royal Garrison Artillery firing 8-inch howitzers. https://s3-ap-southeast-2.amazonaws.com/awm-media/collection/RCDIG1003989/large/4908375.JPG

3 AWM48/6/12 PART2 – December 1917. https://www.awm.gov.au/collection/C1342567?image=65

James Lionel Montague Sandy

James Sandy went to Newington College at Stanmore, NSW, a single-sex college run by the Protestant Church. The College was established in 1863 as the Wesleyan Collegiate Institute. In 1869 it established a Cadet Corps. Over 600 Old Newingtonians enlisted in WWI.

Sandy enlisted in 1914, and went to Egypt as a Second Lieutenant in the 1 Field Artillery Brigade. He served at Gallipoli until he developed blood poisoning after a haemorrhoid operation. This infection caused problems with his ankle that prevented him from running or walking long distances. Recommended for discharge, he applied to join the Flying Corps. After being accepted he returned to Australia to undergo pilot training at the Australian Central Flying School, Point Cook, Victoria. After initial pilot training he returned to the UK on HMT Ulysses, arriving on 28 December 1916. He continued training at No. 23 Training Wing, RFC, until No. 69 Squadron was formed. Assigned to the Squadron he went with the Squadron when it moved to France in August 1917, as Deputy Flight Commander of A Flight. His regular aircraft was R.E.8 No. A3816 and he had several forced landings due to engine trouble. He was a senior experienced pilot in the squadron at the time of his death.

Left: Photograph of Lt Sandy. (Royal Aeronautical Society).

Henry Francis Hughes

Hughes, from Prahran in Melbourne, Victoria, joined the AFC on 21 August 1916, as 2/AM. He was 26 at the time. He had served in the Cadet Corps and a year in the Citizen Military Forces. He travelled to the UK aboard HMT Ulysses on 25 October 1916. He must have been well thought of as he was appointed as temporary Corporal for the trip. In February 1916, he volunteered for training as an air gunner. Promoted to Sergeant in August 1917, he completed courses in the UK before returning to No. 3 Squadron on 10 December. He was making his first combat flight with the squadron on 17 December.

Sandy had been recommended for the Military Cross, and Hughes for the Distinguished Conduct Medal for their action, but the recommendations could not be approved posthumously, and neither was granted.

4 No. 3 Squadron War Diary.
5 Wrigley, H.N. *The Battle Below. Being the history of No. 3 Squadron A.F.C.* Reprint of the 1935 edition. P.44.
6 No. 3 Squadron War Diary.
7 The College only introduced co-education in 2023.
8 His name is also spent Clausz as translated by P.M. Grosz.
9 Letter. R. Ross to R. Waugh. 19.04.1967.
10 R.F.C. Report of Casualties to Personnel and Machines (When Flying), dated 17.12.1917. Copy in author's collection. The loss was reported in RFC Communique No. 118.
11 Col T. Griffiths to Secretary, War Office. 31 Dec 1917. TNA AIR1/1142.

The Duellists

Above: R.E.8 No. A3662 of No. 3 Squadron with the white circle marking that was used by the Squadron from their arrival in France to 22 March 1918.

The R.E.8 Reconnaissance Biplane

The aircraft that No. 3 Squadron, AFC, took into combat was the Royal Aircraft Factory R.E.8. This aircraft had a bad reputation. The hastily trained pilots of No. 52 Squadron, RFC, could not handle the idiosyncrasies of the machine, and several accidents occurred that so demoralised the Squadron personnel that it exchanged its R.E.8 biplanes for the B.E.2c biplanes of No. 34 Squadron in January 1917, it presumably being thought that the more experienced crews of No. 34 could handle the R.E.8.

The combat debut of the R.E.8 was disappointing. On 13 April 1917, six R.E.8 aircraft of No. 59 Squadron were attacked by six Albatros D.III scouts of *Jasta* 11 led by the redoubtable Manfred von Richthofen. All six British aircraft were shot down, only two of the 12 crew surviving.

These early R.E.8s, *especially in the hands of new pilots, had a marked tendency to spin, and there were many fatal accidents at home and overseas, before this tendency was checked by adjustments in the design.*[1]

When the AFC personnel arrived in the UK they underwent a period of rigorous training. No. 3 Squadron went to South Carlton, Lincolnshire, for training with the 23rd Training Wing, RFC. Their training lasted as long as eight months, which was a far different situation from the desperate days of 1917's 'Bloody April.' Some personnel were sent to France to obtain practical experience with serving RFC Squadrons, Sandy being one of these officers. When

Above: Gerald Muir's painting of the last flight of Sandy and Hughes. This painting was reproduced in Wrigley's history of No. 3 Squadron, *The Battle Below.*

No. 3 Squadron flew to France, Sandy was deputy leader of 'A' Flight.

Jack Treacy had amassed a grand total of 113 hours 37 minutes in the air by the time he joined No. 3 Squadron in the field in February 1918. He recalled that although termed an observer, the second member of the R.E.8's crew was a gunner. It was the pilot *who did the actual observing and signalling. Your aerial gunner is watching for the enemy and he lets you know if you are about to be attacked. Photos were taken with a camera behind the gunner's seat. The camera for oblique and map making plates was automatically driven and changed plates itself. All the pilot had to do was to count the time for exposure and overlap on his stopwatch and press the button, the camera did the rest itself. The aerial gunner would change the magazines in the camera on signal from the pilot.*

Treacy stated that in the right hands the R.E.8 *was pretty hot stuff and would fight off two or three (Germans). The only*

Above: A posed photograph of a No. 3 Squadron, AFC, R.E.8 with the white circle insignia.

way to fight with an R.E.8 was to go into a circle when attacked. You tip up on your side and put your engine on full and as soon as the fellow dived you pulled the stick back and made the circle tight. The German can't get inside and your man can stand and fire. You could always turn inside a fighter.[2]

Sandy and Hughes' action illustrates how the Australians made the R.E.8 an effective fighting machine.

The Albatros D.Va

The Albatros D.Va was the last one to enter service, of a line of fighters from Albatros that started with the D.I of 1916. This single seat tractor was powered by a Mercedes six-cylinder in-line engine of 160-hp and equipped with two synchronised machine guns. It was quickly followed by the D.II. The success of the Nieuport sesquiplanes led to the Germans copying the French design. Albatros introduced their D.III 'V-strutter' that employed a small chord lower wing and vee-type interplane struts. The next fighter in the series was the D.V which was basically a lightened D.III. The wing layout was almost the same as the earlier aircraft with the fuselage adopting a nearly elliptical cross section. This model was committed to large scale production, 900 being ordered, but in July 1917, *Idflieg* stated that no more were to be built, only the D.III. This remarkable turnaround was caused by repeated wing failures of the D.V.

In order to salvage as much of the D.V program as possible Albatros modified the D.V to produce the D.Va.

This new aircraft is *practically the same in external appearance as the D.5, but of much stronger construction. This type was probably designed owing to instances of the D.5 breaking up in the air. The D.5a, however, is much heavier than the D.5, and even heavier than the old D.3, which means that its performance, especially in the climb, will be much reduced.*[3]

The only external identifying feature was the return to the aileron control of the D.III..[4] Fortunately the more powerful 180-hp Mercedes D.IIIa engine became available to give the D.Va a performance to match the newer Allied fighters. Wing failure still occurred and the problem was to stay with the Albatros D.Va throughout its life as a complete 'fix' was never achieved.

Some 1,612 Albatros D.Va fighters were ordered by October 1917. Albatros fighters peaked at the front in April 1918; - 928 D.Va; 131 D.V and 174 D.III fighters being recorded out of a total of 1,949 fighters.[5] The D.Va was the last Albatros fighter to be produced in quantity, for although Albatros produced designs and prototypes up to the D.XII, none achieved a production order. Albatros continued to build fighters receiving large orders for the Fokker D.VII.

D.5390/17 was one of a batch of 262 (D.5165/17 to D.5426/17) ordered in August 1917.[6]

Royal Prussian *Jagdstaffel* 29

Jasta 29 was formed at *Flieger-Ersatz-Abteilung* 5 (Aviation Replacement Section 5) in Hannover on 28 December 1916.

Above: Possibly the prototype Albatros D.V with the headrest for the pilot. This was soon removed as the pilot's complained it interfered with their rear vision. The aileron controls may be seen, with the removal of the headrest, this was the only external difference between the D.V and the D.Va. The aircraft has been painted in a pattern mimicking the lozenge fabric.

Above: Believed to be outside the Albatros works at Johannisthal, D5390/17 is in its factory makings. Note the weights legend, fuselage cross and serial number on the fin. The rudder is covered in lozenge fabric.

Above & Below: D.5390/17 during its recovery by No. 3 Squadron, AFC. (John Joshua Collection. nla-4900884)

Above, Below, & Following Page: D.5390/17 was reassembled on the field of No. 3 Squadron and these photographs taken at that time. They ended up in the photographic albums of many of No. 3 Squadron's personnel who survived the war. Note the tailplane overpainting. No photograph of the port side seems to have survived from this photographic set. (AHT AL0068-05 & 06)

Above: The over-painted tailplane is well shown in this view, as is the replacement losenge fabric starboard aileron.

Above: D.5390/17 in British markings. Note how the weights legend has been revealed by scraping the paint off the fuselage.

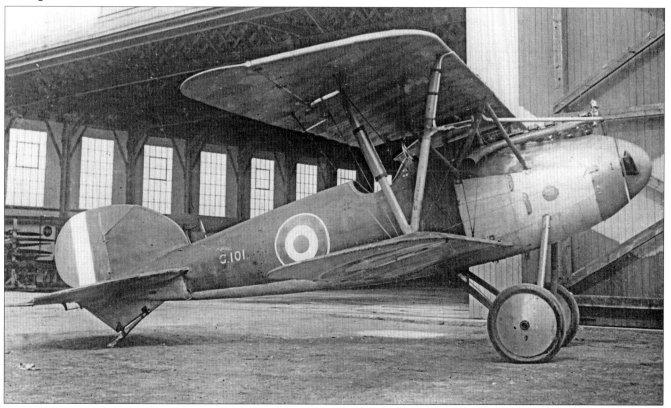

Above: G.101 was the serial applied to the Albatros by the British. The roundels have a white outline. A pitot has been fitted for testing by the British. Note the stencilling on the interplane V-strut.

Above: On display in Australia House in the UK with incorrect German crosses added. Considering the number of times the fighter was broken down and reassembled, it is amazing that it did not suffer more damage before arriving in Australia.

At the end of the war its personnel had been awarded 79 victories. The *Jasta*, with Pfalz and Albatros fighters, had transferred to the area several weeks earlier to the combat with Sandy and Hughes, to assist the German 6 *Armee* and were based at Bellincamps.[7]

The Australian squadrons in this sector would often encounter the Albatros and Pfalz scouts of *Jasta* 29. No. 4 Squadron, AFC, had its first combat with *Jasta* 29 on 13 January 1918. A patrol of No.4 Squadron's Sopwith Camel fighters ran into the *Jasta's* scouts and Lt F.B. Willmott in B5602 was cut off from his companions and forced to land in enemy lines becoming a PoW. This victory was credited to *Ltn* Shuster.

A combined raid on the ammunition dump at Armentieres by the bombers of No. 110 Squadron, RAF, escorted by No. 4 Squadron's Camels took place on 18 May 1918. As the formation turned for home it was attacked by about 30 Albatros and Pfalz scouts. Lt O.C. Barry in Camel B7480 fell in flames to the guns of *Uffz* Pech of *Jasta* 29 for Pech's eighth victory. The Australians claimed one Albatros out of control in the fight. The combat ended with the formation scattered all over the sky. As the Allied aircraft tried to reach their lines, a thick fog blanketed the ground. Not one aircraft made its home airfield. No 4 Squadron was fortunate that no one was killed in the resultant forced

landings; the British squadrons losing two pilots killed in attempting to land.

Jasta 29 was credited with 96 victories, with 13 killed, 12 wounded in action, two killed and one wounded in flying accidents and one PoW.[8]

Ltn d Res **Rudolf Clauss**

The German pilot of D.5329/17, the 24 year old *Ltn* Rudolph Carl Hermann Clauss, managed to land his scout on fairly level ground in front of the trenches that housed members of the 21st Battalion. On this cold day of 17 December, the men were engaged on cleaning out and deepening their trenches. Maj Alf Reed was in charge of a company of the 21st when *a German plane disengaged itself from the fight & to my surprise it landed close to my dugout. Before the pilot had time to destroy it, we seized him & I placed a guard over the plane, which on examination proved to have only a small hole in the petrol tank through which the petrol had escaped.*

The pilot, a young German officer wearing an Iron Cross, was brought to my dug-out & I advised Brigade Hqrs of what had occurred. The prisoner had a flesh-wound in one leg caused by shrapnel from one of the "archies". We dressed the wound after we had searched him. During the night a party under Captain R Ross, no 60 Squadron AFC, arrived & dismantled the plane

COMITÉ INTERNATIONAL DE LA CROIX-ROUGE

RES/ARCH/serv.brit/ace

Geneva, 18 september 2001

CERTIFICATE

The Central Tracing Agency has received the following information:

Name, first name	: CLAUSS Rudolf Carl Hermann
Date of birth	: 18.8.1893
Place of birth	: Stauchitz
Father's name	: not indicated
Rank	: Lt.
Unit	: Not indicated
Date and place of capture	: 17.12.1917 at Armentière
Serial number	: 159130
Place (s) of internment	: interned in "Spn 26966" (Bevois Mount and Skating Rink, Southampton) (according to information dated 4.1.1918)
From	: one list from the British authorities

International Committee of the Red Cross
CENTRAL TRACING AGENCY
— GENEVA —

which was packed on a tender & taken away.[9]

Clauss had been awarded one aerial victory to the time of his capture. This was for an R.E.8 claimed west of Blankaartsee in Belgium on 13 November 1917. There are no British losses recorded on this day. Clauss was the only PoW from *Jasta* 29.

Clauss was born on18 August 1893, at Grauswitz in Saxony. His parents were landowners and he was engaged in farm work in Baravia after completing his schooling. Prior to being called up for his compulsory military service in the Bavarian Army, Clauss enlisted as a one-year volunteer. He had four weeks left of his military service when the war broke out and his artillery unit was mobilised.

In October 1914, he was awarded the Iron Cross (2nd Class) and promoted to *Vizefeldwebel* some weeks later. He transferred to the Saxon Army in March 1915, and was promoted to *Leutnant des Reserve* on 16 May 1915, while with *Field Art Rgt* 115. He was wounded and spent some time in hospital. After this he applied for the air service and began his training at Hannover in January 1916. He received his pilot's certification on 31 October 1916.[10]

Clauss was with *Armee Flug Park* (*AFP*) 1 on 13 June 1917. The AFPs were immediately behind the front line and provided replacements to units that required personnel. The number refers to the *Armee* to which they were attached. Clauss was immediately transferred to *Jasta* 29.

From 21 June to 6 August 1917, Clauss was on sick leave from *Jasta* 29.

On 6 August 1917, Clauss was posted to *Flieger Ersatz* (*FEA*) 5. The FEAs were replacement units well behind the lines. *FEA* 5 was at Hannover and carried out training and replacements to the *AFPs*. *FEA* 5 commenced before the start of hostilities and remained at Hannover until the end of the war.

The same day Clauss was posted to *Kampf-Einsitzer Staffel* (*KESt*) 1a at Mannheim, remaining with this unit until 26 October when he was re-posted to *Jasta* 29. The *KESt* units were employed for Home Defence. This is thought to have been an administrative move to clean up the paperwork as Clauss could not be in Hannover and Mannheim on the same day.

Clauss had the following Saxon decorations: Knights Cross 2nd Class with Swords of the Albrecht Order 15 January 1917; Knights Cross 2nd Class with Swords of Saxon Merit Order 1 My 1917.

Clauss was vague during his interrogation. His wounds were addressed and he was interned in *"Spn 26966" (Bevois Mount and Skating Rink, Southampton).*[11] His woollen lined flying boots were souvenired by Alf Reed who donated them to the AWM in the 1920.[12]

Little else is known about Clauss. It appears that he returned to Germany after the war and served in the Luftwaffe in WWII, where he was s supply officer in a training squadron. He died from injuries from an aircraft accident on 15 October 1941.[13]

The Recovery

Roderick Ross recalled that *During the night of the day on which this fight occurred, I personally took a team practically up to the front line near Armentiers, took the German plane to pieces and collected the wounded German pilot and brought them back to our squadron aerodrome at Baillieul. The night was extremely cold and as we took the German plane apart working by means of the flashes from one of our 4.5 howitzer batteries a little further back, the cooling liquid from the radiator froze as it dropped onto the bottom wing.*

Regarding the German Pilot. He was not wounded in the foot but was wounded on the inside of the leg high up near his crutch. Although somewhat painful, he could walk quite well and without any limp.[14]

Sgt Francis Latimer of No. 3 Squadron wrote that *8 men were sent out to within rifle distance of line to salvage Hun machine & brought it in alright this morning. Machine absolutely intact & good prize. Much interest in racy looking bus. Machine roughly put together again before being sent off to depot and photographed by Major's orders.*[15] The depot was No. 1 Aircraft Depot at St Omer, and was received by *Riggers at Repair Park No. 1 A S D,* on 18.12.1917.[16] The Australians realised that the aircraft would have to be examined and tested by the British as it was the first of its type to fall into British hands, but they immediately put in a claim for the machine as a war prize.

Ross' official report on the recovery noted that the machine had been successfully landed after having its petrol tank shot through and *was in otherwise perfect condition.*

On taking over the aeroplane from the guard supplied by "A" Coy., 21st Battn., 2nd Aus. Division. I was informed that a watch had been stolen from the machine.

The engine is a Mercedes of 160 H.P. made by Daimler (German) No.33842. The following markings are stamped on crankcase in ½" type:
BN627 MN43
GARANTIE. BIS. 1.3.18.
Two "Spandau" Machine Guns Nos. 7778 and 7969 are fitted and synchronised with the propellor. They also bear the following marking:
LMG 08/15
G.W.F.
SPANDAU
1917

The propellor No. 16969 is of 9 laminations and is by Garuda.

The following instruments are carried:
Watch (removed before arrival of Flying Corps).
Revolution Indicator No. 84949 by Wilhelm Morill (*sic*) of Leipzig
Petrol Gauge – Bosch No. 48092.
Oil Pressure Gauge – By Maximall of Berlin.

Experiment and Research

Summary of Report No. M.180, March, 1918. Trials of Albatross (*sic*) Scout, No. G.101

Type – Single-seater Scout
Engine – 160 H.P. Mercedes
Propeller – Garuda Feld Propeller, 1914, 2-bladed tractor
      Diam. 2805. Pitch 1815
Number of crew – One
Military Duty – Fighting scout
*Total military load – 281 lbs.

	M.P.H.	Revs.
Speed at 10000 ft.	105½	1410 (approx.)
Speed at 15000 ft.	97	1340

Rate of Climb in I.A.S.

Mins.	Secs.	Ft./min.	M.P.H.	Revs.
Climb to 10000 ft.				
16	30	400	65	1315
Climb to 15000 ft.				
35	35	165	59	1285

Service ceiling, 16,500 ft. (Height at rate of climb is 100 ft. per min.)
Estimated absolute ceiling, 18,500 ft.
Greatest height reached, 16,000 ft. in 42 mins. 30 secs.
Rate of climb at this height, 120 ft. per min.
Total weight of machine fully loaded, 2,031 obs.
Weight per sq. ft., 8.6 lbs. Weight per H.P., 12.7 lbs.
Total military load made up as follows:

Pilot	180 lbs.
Two Spandau guns and ammunition	101 lbs.
	281 lbs.

The performance of this machine is practically the same as that of Albatross (*sic*) Scout No. G.56, with 160 H.P. Mercedes engine. (See Report No. M.154.)

Owing to the position in which the bullet entered the petrol tank. It was only possible to salve the remaining two gallons of petrol. Samples of oil and radiator water are held awaiting instructions. The radiator water is not anti-freezing.[17]

The machine was erected, trued up & checked; Tanks fitted tested & refitted; New left hand shock absorber fitted: pitot head & tubing fitted by 2 January 1918, and handed over to Home Establishment on the 6th, and was flown on the 13, 15, 17, 19, 21 January for a total of 7 hours 55 minutes *since overhaul.*[18]

On the 18th February *Repairing Prop* was recorded. At some stage the original Garuda airscrew was replaced by a British one.

The British Log Book for G.101 reveals that it was removed from Lympe on 13 January 1918. Dispatched by air to Hendon where it was recorded as having 160-hp Mercedes engine No. BN627 date stamped 11.3.18.[19] Claimed as a War Prize by the Australian Government D.5390/17 was taken over by the AFC on 22 May. On the 25th, *Machine dismantled Engine removed from fuselage Machine packed for export overseas.* The aircraft had recorded 14 hours three minutes flying time in British hands.[20] The Armistice saw a display of war material held at Australia House, The Strand, London, that opened on 2 December 1918, and D.5390/17 took pride of place in the exhibition.[21]

Endnotes:

1 Owers, C.A. 'Memories of Number 3 Squadron, A.F.C. An interview with Jack Treacy by Colin A Owers.' *14-18 Journal 1972-73.* ASWWIAF, Sydney, 1972. P.4.
2 Jack Treacy interview. *Op Cit.*
3 'Albatros Scout.' *Technical Review of German Aeroplanes brought down in our Lines on the Western Front during 1917.* April 1918. TNA AIR1/910/204/5/831.
4 The British noted in their test of Albatros D.V (D.2129/17) British No. G.56 that *On account of the number of accidents with this machine, which was probably too weak, the Germans have evidently been obliged to strengthen it.* 'Enemy Aviation for the Month of January, 1918.' Ministry of Munitions. April 1918. TNA MUN4/5010.
5 Grosz, P.M. 'The Agile and Aggressive Albatros.' *Air Enthusiast Quarterly,* No.1. (1974), UK. P.38.
6 *Ibid.* P.48.
7 The story of *Jasta 29* can be found in *The Jasta Pilots* by Franks, Bailey and Duiven (Grub Street Publications, UK. 1996).
8 *Ibid.*
9 'Details of the capture of the Memorial's Albatros D.Va.' AWM Hall of Fame information Sheet by C. Goddard.
10 For more details of Clauss' pre-aviation career see Pegram, Dr A. 'The Last Flight of the Albatros.' *14-18 Journal.* 2022 P.20.
11 Certificate from International Red Cross. 18.09.2001.
12 AWM 93 File 7/4/532.
13 Pegram, A. *Op Cit.*
14 Letter. R. Ross to R. Waugh. 19.04.1967.
15 Sgt F. Latimer. AWM Private Record PR84/22.
16 British Log Book.
17 R Ross. No. 69 Sqn, AFC. In the Field. 18.12.17.
18 British Log Book.
19 Temporary Log Book Albatross (*sic*) Scout G101 160 HP Mercedes No BN627/MN43. AWM 25 Item
20 British Log Book. The engine was recorded as having run 16 hrs 37 mins.
21 AWM File No. 981/3. However, AWM File 90/0313 states that the display was in early 1918 with the aircraft then packed for shipment.

Albatros D.5390/17 in Australia

Above: The Albatros on display with Parer and McIntosh's de Havilland D.H.9 in the background. The Albatros is still in good condition and the lozenge fabric may be clearly seen under the top wing. The location is unknown as both aircraft were displayed at Melbourne and Sydney before moving to the Aeroplane Hall in the newly opened AWM in 1941.

This Page, Facing Page Below The restored D.5390/17 on display at Camden airfield. The major error in the colour scheme is the overall lozenge fabric and the addition of a fuselage cross.

This Page & Facing Page:
The return of the Albatros
to the AWM by RAAF C-130
Hercules

Shipped to Australia with other war trophies on the *Booral*, the Albatros was displayed in the Exhibition Building in Melbourne in 1920, and then in the Motor Trader's Association of South Australia's exhibition in Adelaide in October 1920. The Albatros returned to Melbourne on 30 November 1920, and was displayed at the Melbourne and Sydney Exhibition Buildings until 1941, when it was moved to the Aeroplane Hall in the newly opened AWM in Canberra.

First Restoration

Memorial staff had carried out work in patching and varnishing the original fabric and structure at various times between its acquisition and 1965. These repairs could be

Above: D.5390/17 on display. Note how the fuselage colour tends towards brown.

readily identified as they used red dope and pinked edge fabric patches. Neither were employed by either side in WWI. A large patch on the upper surface of the top wing was the largest single repair to the fabric surfaces. The original fabric to the fore and aft of this patch was still present, and enabled the pattern of the fabric to be worked out for this location.

In the early 1960s the D.Va and Pfalz D.XII were moved into storage in one of the old sheds at Duntroon.[1] These sheds were not ideal for the storage of such historical items. The Australian Society of WWI Aero Historians arranged for Mr Harold Thomas of the Camden Museum of Aviation to undertake a restoration of the Albatros *to its original captured condition*[2], and the aircraft was flown in a RAAF Lockheed Hercules to Camden on 29 June 1966.[3] The Albatros was flown back to Canberra in a Hercules transport on 21 May 1968.[4]

The wings, control surfaces were stripped of fabric. The ply fuselage was rubbed back and revarnished.[5] Holes in the fuselage were blocked and glued from the inside to preserve the original woodwork. The spinner was hammered back into shape and the metal panels treated and repainted. The exhaust manifold was missing and the RAAF made a copy from an original in the AWM's collection. The restored fuselage as given several coats of dark green paint.

The 'restoration' was said to have taken in excess of 2,000 manhours by volunteers. The fuselage was scraped, sanded and repaired and given two coats of wood preserver and two coats of wood preserver and one coat of marine varnish.

Lozenge pre-printed fabric was not available at the time and the five-colour shapes had to be duplicated in a stencil for each colour, and each colour was sprayed using thermofax fabric water dye. To spray the 130 feet of fabric took many weeks, as no two adjoining colours could be applied at the same time, and the water-based dye had a long drying time.

All steel parts were cleaned and zinc-chromated. Unfortunately, using untrained volunteers the restoration had many problems.[6] No work was done on preserving the original paint.[7] The colour scheme applied was not that carried by the machine when captured. Other problems were to come to light in future years.

In 1996 it was discovered that the original fittings that held the spinner in place had evidently been lost when the aircraft had been at Camden. The missing parts held the spinner in place over the rear plate. The back plate is a large and flimsy sheet metal component. During restoration the lack of this item had been overcome by the restorers by reversing the back plate, roughly hammering it flat so it would fit against the airscrew. As the Albatros had significant problems at this time: - an inaccurate colour scheme,

Above: D.9450/17 on display in the Aeroplane Hall at the AWM with Lancaster 'G for Geroge' in the background.

incorrect fabric, oil soakage to the fuselage, incorrect engine[8] and an incorrect airscrew, it was proposed to leave the spinner problem until the machine could go through the workshop for a through conservation effort. The machine was left on display in the Aeroplane Hall without the spinner until 1999.

Second Restoration

The AWM decided to establish a display in the new ANZAC Hall for the centenary of WWI. This was to be entitled 'Over the Front' and was to include all five of the AWM's WWI aircraft, the Albatros D.Va, Pfalz D.XII. S.E.5a, Avro 504K, and the de Havilland D.H.9, the last being the machine flown, or rather flown between a series of crashes, by Ray Parer and John McIntosh from the UK to Australia in 1920.[9] Although a civil aircraft, this machine is practically the same as those flown in WWI, but lacking armament and a radiator, the latter having been replaced by one from a car that was installed after one of its crashes.[10]

The Albatros had been on display after its restoration in the 1960s, and a number of areas required attention. There was a significant accumulation of dust, dirt, grease and the discoloured shellac layer applied by the last restoration that had to be removed from the fuselage. The wing fabric had contracted placing considerable strain on the structure of the wings including deformation of the trailing edge. As fabric that had been printed with the original pattern was now

available, and the hand painted fabric on the aircraft did not look realistic, it was decided to replace all the fabric with the newly available fabric. The correct Mercedes engine, No. BN627/33842, would be installed in the machine at this time.

The aircraft were removed to the AWM' Treloar Technology Centre. In order to carry out the work on the Albatros a special rotating steel frame was built to enable work to be carried out without damage to the machine. The Albatros was built using a pre-formed ply shell that was attached to 14 formers and three longerons on each side to give a strong light structure. As the ply could not be removed this method of working was adopted for the fuselage. Where damage to the ply fuselage had been patched, these were removed and replaced with a fitted ply piece with a glued reinforcing plate of minimum dimensions to restore the original finish and not to intrude onto the original material more than absolutely necessary.

Outside expertise was brought in where required. The Germans developed a pre-printed fabric towards the end of the war. It was in two patterns, one of four colours and the other of five colours. Each pattern had light colours for undersurfaces and dark for upper surfaces. Sometimes the light colour was used on both surfaces. The original rollers that produced this fabric had survived and the dyes were still manufactured. The AWM obtained the correct pattern for the restoration of the Albatros and Pfalz D.XII scouts.

Above: John White and helper spreading the original fabric out for inspection.

Above & Below Left: The Albatros fuselage suspended on a rotating frame to allow work to be done without damage to the machine.

Right: The rotating frame allowed detail photographs to be taken of the interior.

Above: The Albatros was not the only aircraft being readied for the 'Over the Front' display. This ex-RAAF S.E.5a was donated to the AWM and has been restored in AFC colours even though it embodies late RAAF modifications.

Above: The wings were mounted on these frames so that they could be repaired before being covered in appropriate fabric – newly printed lozenge fabric where required for the Albatros.

Above: Wings mounted on frames so that they could be repaired.

Below: Another view of the work area at the AWM's Mitchell facility.

Above: The Albatros upper wing covered in plain fabric just like it had when completed by the Albatros factory.

Above & Left: Views showing how the metal frame was bolted to the Albatros engine bearers.

Above, Above Right, Below, & Below Right: The fuselage of the Albatros was mounted in this frame so that it could be rotated to allow access to every part without placing undue stress on the fuselage structure.

Above & Above Right: The bottom of the fuselage was exposed to minute examination. The discolouration was caused by oil leaking through from the engine.

Above: This view up the engine bay shows how access was provided using the rotating frame.

Above & Below Left: This photograph shows how the Camden restoration colours were rubbed back to reveal the series of colours applied to the machine.

Above, Below Left, Below, Facing Page Above Left: The recovery of the original fabric made the restoration to replicate the machine's appearance when captured easier. The material was in various states of preservation as may be seen.

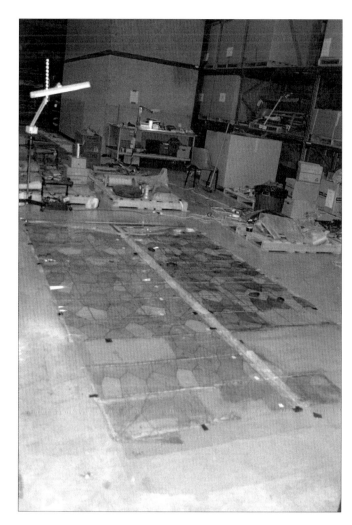

Above & Below: Detail shots sowing the work done to establish the correct colour for metal work.

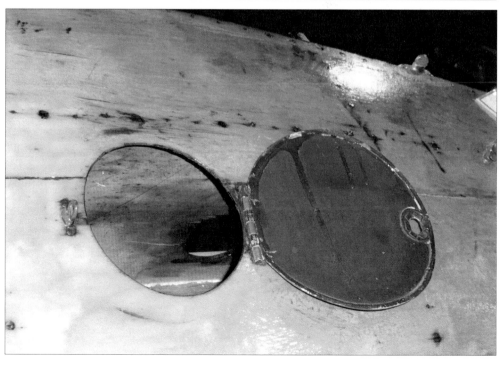

Right: Hatch under fuselage.

Above: The two restored WWI warbirds waiting for their roll out.

Above: Debuted to the press and waiting admirers.

Below: Being prepared for having their photographs taken..

Above: D.5390/17 has the fuselage cross and the serial number on the fin overpainted just like it was when brought down by No. 3 Squadron, AFC, on that fateful December day in 1917.

Above: The weights legend was applied to replicate how it was when in British hands.

Above, Below, & Facing Page: Vews of the restored Albatros.

Above: Rear view showing the camouflage pattern on the wings. The photographs on No. 3 Squadron's airfield show that the tailplane was overpainted but this was not reproduced in this restoration.

Endnotes

1. Another reference states that the Albatros was at Duntroon since 1955. 'Albatros D Va of the Australian War Memorial.' AHSA Journal. May–June 1966. P.42.
2. Letter AWM to N. Hewitt, ASWWIAH. 24.05.1966.
3. Parnell, N.M. 'An Albatros in Australia.' *Air Pictorial*. April 1968. P.125.
4. Cranston, F. 'An Albatros Makes Its Last Flight.' *Canberra Times*, Wednesday 22 May 1969.
5. The author is ashamed to admit that he was one of those who sanded the fuselage without thought of trying to preserve the original finish and markings. Restorations by amateurs need a strong oversight by professional staff to ensure that all details are recorded and preserved.
6. Cutting from *Aircraft* magazine. No date.
7. The author spent one Saturday afternoon sanding the fuselage, not having any background on aircraft preservation at that time, did not realise I was destroying historical material.
8. Mercedes engine No. 627/33842 was removed from public exhibition and installed in the Pfalz D.XII 2600/18 by the ASWWIAP who were restoring the D.XII at this time. Unfortunately, the Society used oil in the engine and this leaked such that the Pfalz structure became weak and could not hold the weight of an engine. It is presently fitted with a mock-up of a Mercedes engine.
9. The story of all the aircraft, Allied and German, brought back to Australia after WWI see Owers, C. 'Australia's First Museum.' *Air Enthusiast* No.47, Key Publishing, UK. P.28.
10. The story in his own words - Parer, R.J.P. *Flight and Adventures of Parer and McIntosh – by air from England to Australia 1919*. Reprint. Messenger, Vic, 1986.

The Wings

Above & Below: The upper wing as delivered to the Camden Aviation Museum.

Upper Wing

The upper one-piece wing is constructed mainly of timber around two box spars, with a number of steel fittings. The ribs appear to be made as a mass production set as they have position numbers marked on them. The ribs are constructed of light timber with ply capping strips and ply reinforcing strips. Eight steel compression tubes are mounted between the spars, and they are joined by wire cross bracing cables. At five positions on the spars, reinforcement has been applied by means of wrapping the spar in cord and consolidating this with glue. The top plywood leading edge was added after the front spar was reinforced.

A rear beam carries the ailerons and runs across the wing except where the cutout for the pilot's vision.

There are 14 ribs on the port side and 13 on the starboard due to the radiator's position. The two radiator support ribs are of thicker cross section.

The trailing edge was a piano wire approximately 1 mm in diameter, and attached to each rib by an aluminium clip. This gives the wings their scalloped appearance after the fabric shrinks under the action of doping the fabric.

The wing had suffered damage over the years and subjected to a substantial repair. Red dope had been applied

to the upper surface of the mainplane. This occurred before 1965 and was probably carried out as the only material available. It is not a German treatment.

The upper wing had a covering of plain un-printed fabric, while the lower surface was the five-colour light lozenge fabric. This was applied first, the upper surface fabric was then applied, the trailing edge fabric wrapped over the lower surface, sewn in position and trimmed to give about a 10 mm overlap. Plain fabric rib tapes 10 mm wide were applied to the upper surface. On the lower surface the rib tapes were 7 and 10 mm and purple in colour. The 7 mm tapes were used only on the ribs adjacent to the wing radiator. 30 mm wide purple tape was used to seal the leading and trailing edges.

Strips of lozenge fabric were applied to many locations as a means of reducing chafing. Some of these remained at the time of the 2008 conservation.

After removal of the fabric from the 1960s 'restoration', extensive damage to a number of ribs was discovered. It appeared that this damage was done during the 'restoration.'[32]

Ailerons

The ailerons are constructed of welded steel tube with a number of timber fittings. The construction follows the rib

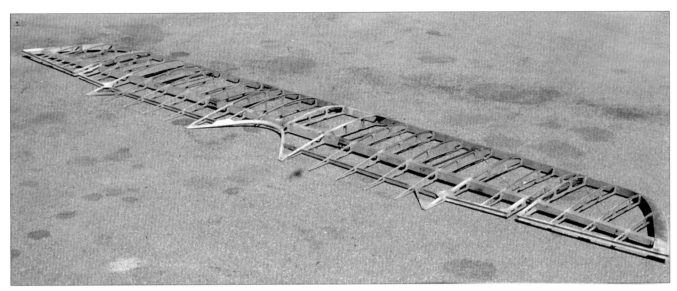

Above: The stripped upper wing at Camden.

Above & Above Right: Top and bottom views of the stripped upper wing.

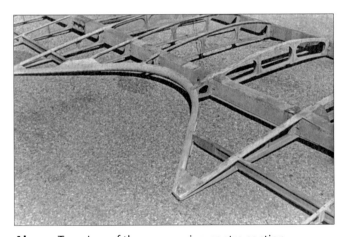

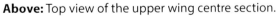

Above: Top view of the upper wing centre section.

Above: Centre section at AWM during restoration.

spacing positions. Five hinge straps are retained in place by profiled timber blocks held by two screws. These blocks also anchor the fabric covering to the frame. The entire steel aileron frame was painted with a flat grey primer. It appears that paper chafing strips were applied to replace the original fabric strips in the 1960 rebuild.

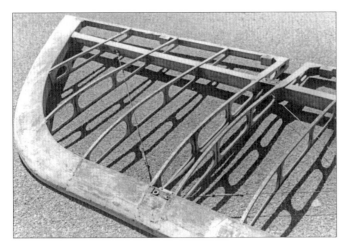

Above: Top view of upper wing showing the aileron lever cut-out.

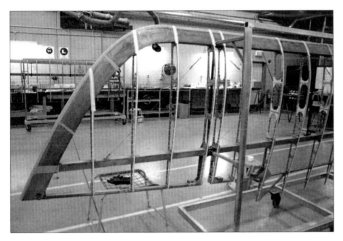

Above & Below: Top and bottom views of the upper wing under restoration at the AWM showing the aileron cut out and compression tube.

Right: Detail of compression tube at aileron cut-out on upper wing.

Above, Above Right, & Below: Aileron details when the aircraft arrived at the Camden Aviation Museum.

Above: View of the welded steel tube aileron without fabric.

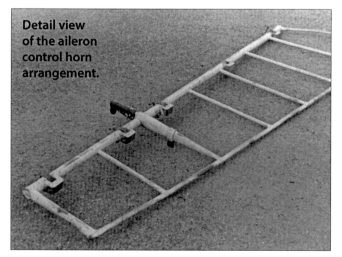

Detail view of the aileron control horn arrangement.

Lower Wings

The lower planes area constructed similar to the upper wing but have only one main spar with three steel tube compression members each. The top of all planes have ply reinforcement leading edge to the front spar.

Port Lower Wing

On the upper surface of the spar is a data block – about 40 mm outboard of Rib 2. This was originally covered by a celluloid cover. The block comprises a stamped Albatros logo, hand written date: 3.8.17 a signature and the ZAK stamp

Above: Aileron horn and hinges on the restored machine, 2023.

Right: Detail of the gap between end of aileron and wing.

Above: Port wings when removed for transport to Camden. The lower wing cross has been overpainted by the British roundel, then a white circle and then a representation of the German cross. The poor condition of the fabric is very noticeable on the upper surface.

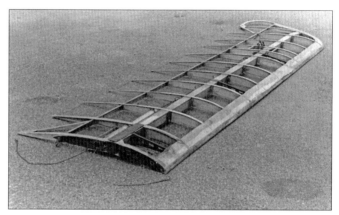

Above: The lower port wing stripped of fabric. The aileron cables may be seen extending from the wing root.

Left: Aileron control cable pulley inside lower wing.

Below Left: View at the port wing root showing the aileron cable tube.

Below: Underside view of restored wing showing the aileron cable tube with its opening for access to join the wires to the control wires passing through the fuselage to the pilot's controls.

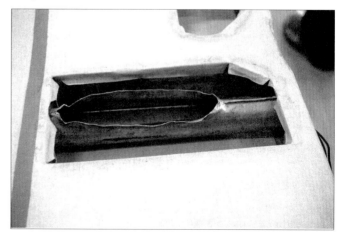

Above: View at the wing root showing the tube for the aileron cables and the hatches for access.

Above: Detail of the lower port wing tip, bottom view.

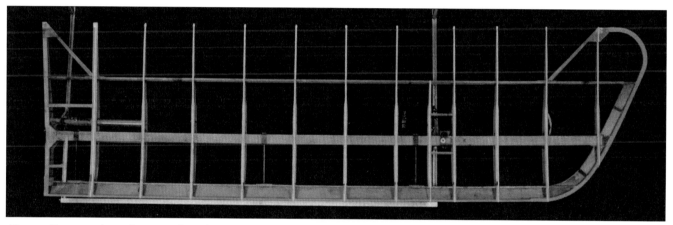

Above: Bottom view of stripped starboard wing.

Above: Port stub wing at fuselage showing attachments and aileron and bracing cable attachments. The original paint work has suffered in its 70 odd years since applied.

Above: The starboard side before restoration.

Above: Port stub wing at fuselage showing attachments and aileron and bracing cable attachments. The original paint work has suffered in its 70 odd years since applied.

Above: Starboard stub wing.

Above & Above Right: The spar attachment before and after the 2008 restoration.

Above: Detail view of aileron control pulley in lower starboard wing. Note that rib tap[es are tacked on both sides of opening.

Above: Starboard lower wing with plain fabric as per the original covering..

Above & Below: The lower wings in storage racks with the upper wing and Caribou wings behind. 2023.

over '9 SEP 1917'.

On the lower surface of both spars is an ink stamp '2765 U.1', indicating that the wings are a matched pair.

Starboard Lower Wing

Original paint was found and removed from the underside of the leading edge. On the front leading edge was a strip of original fabric over 4 m long.

This wing was in very good condition.

The inboard lower aluminium access hatch is fitted with two hinges. This retained paint layers including the original undersurface blue colour.

The trailing edge of all wings had been replaced with thin brass wire. This was replaced with $^1/_{16}$ inch diameter stainless wire.

The lower wings have suffered less damage than the upper wings.

All rib repairs were made with timber of the same thickness and similar density.

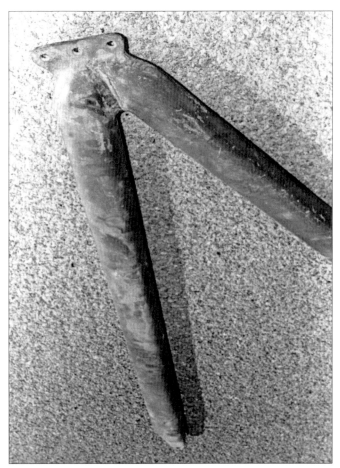

Above & Above Right: Interplane V-struts

Interplane and Cabane struts

The interplane are of two lengths of aerofoil section steel tubes welded into a V shape with welded attachment brackets at the top and bottom.

Right: The cabane struts.

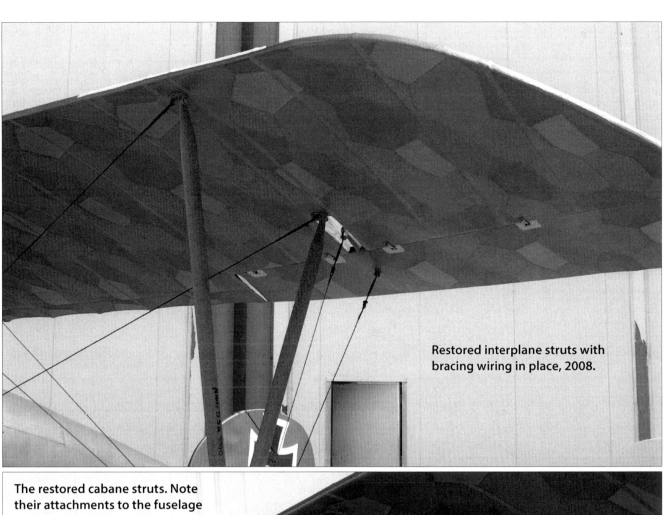

Restored interplane struts with bracing wiring in place, 2008.

The restored cabane struts. Note their attachments to the fuselage and the upper wing, 2008.

Above: Wing bracing cables at wing root.

Above: The footstep along the spar of the lower wing butt up to the rigging plate.

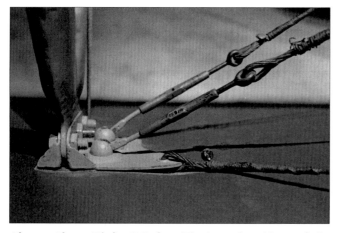

Above, Above Right, & Below: The interplane V-strut fitting includes the bracing fixtures.

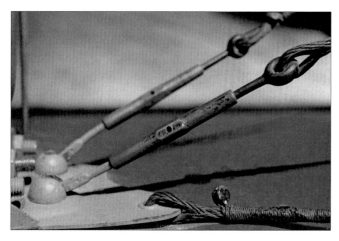

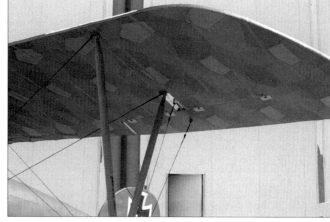

Above & Top 4 Photos, Facing Page: Port and starboard aileron horns and cables. The D.Va had the same aileron operating system as the D.III.

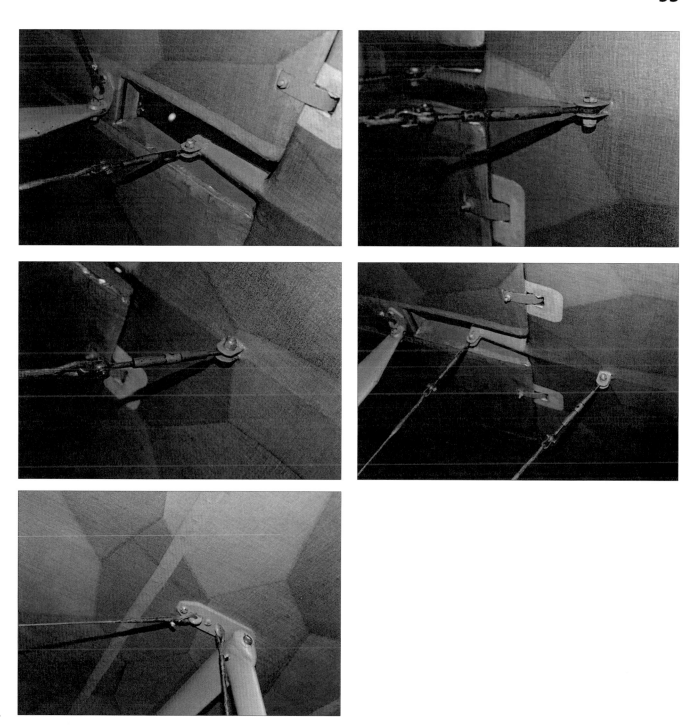

Above: Upper cabane strut connection.

Above: Port This photograph at the Camden Aviation Museum shows the condition of the attachment point on the fuselage at this time. The footstep was added in the later in the restoration.

Above: The same area after its restoration at the Camden Aviation Museum.

Facing Page, Above: Detail of footstep and drift wire attachment point. Note the spring and retaining strap for the cowl panel.

Above: An Albatros data plate for D.Va D.5062/17. The plate is approx 97 mm long.

Facing Page, Below: Starboard drift wire attachment.

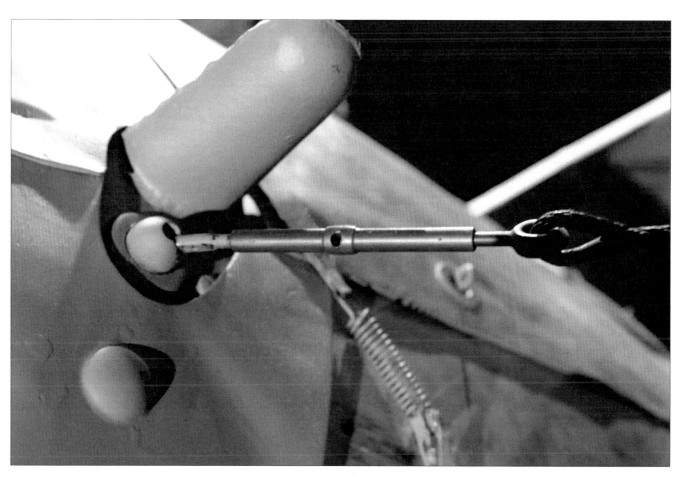

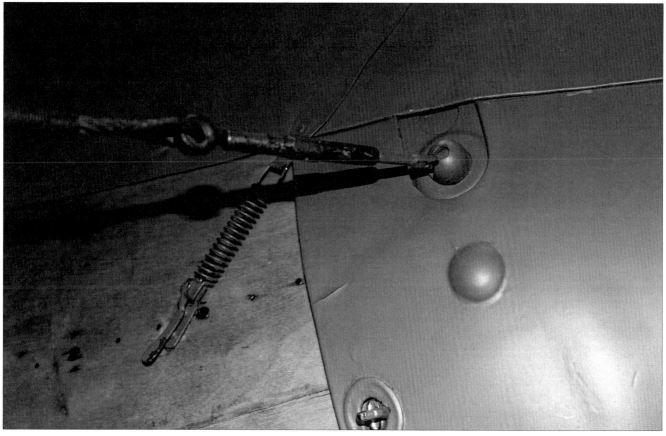

The Aerofoil Radiator

Above & Facing Page, Above: The radiator followed the aerofoil of the upper wing on the bottom surface but raised up from the curve of the ribs at its rear on the upper wing surface.

The radiator fitted to Albatros aircraft from the D.III forward was an aerofoil shaped radiator fitted into the top wing, offset to starboard, such that if it was holed during combat, the water would not spray onto the pilot.

The radiator fitted to D.5390/17 was built by the Daimler Company of Stuttgart. The body of the radiator was fabricated from sheet metal with heavy gauge metal brackets at each corner for attaching it to the front and rear spars. The radiator fits between the first and third ribs on the starboard side of the upper wing.

The radiator followed the wing's shape and the only protuberance was the header tank and this was carefully streamlined to offer the minimum resistance to the airflow over the wing. The bottom of the radiator matches the aerofoil section, but the upper follows a divergent line to be 26 mm above the wing at its rear. Two small connecting pipes for the rubber water pipes to and from the engine are located at the underside of the front starboard corner. They are marked 'EINLAUF' (inlet) and 'AUSLAUF' (outlet). Hot water is pumped up from the engine and circulates through the honeycomb of cooling tubes and then back out to the engine. The cooling tubes are made of a non-ferrous metal and are set in the radiator body at an angle of 45° to the line of flight.

Cooling air is drawn up from below and discharged above the upper wing. This flow is controlled by the pilot who can operate a series of shutters on the lower surface of the radiator block. The shutter is attached by two steel pins. When the shutter is closed, it blocks the flow of air to approximately one half of the radiator, thus enabling the pilot to heat his engine to operating temperature. By opening the shutter cooling air is directed up and through the radiator.

The radiator has the manufacturer's plate on the rear underside and another small plate on the front of the header tank.

FABRIKATIONS	No. 1246 (Fabrication No.)
ZULÄSS. BESCHEING	No. (Registration No.)
	No number on this unit.
TYPE	D.III
ZEICHNUNG No.	47640 (Drawing No.)
WASSERINHALT	11 L (Water capacity in litres)
KÜHLFLÄCHE	114.7 qm[1] (Cooling Area in m^2)
DURCHFLUSSZEIT	100 l - 35 sk[2]

Endnotes:
1. 158 ft^2 approx.
2. 100 litres/35 secs = 38 gal/min approx.

Below: Close-up of the shutters on the lower surface of the radiator.

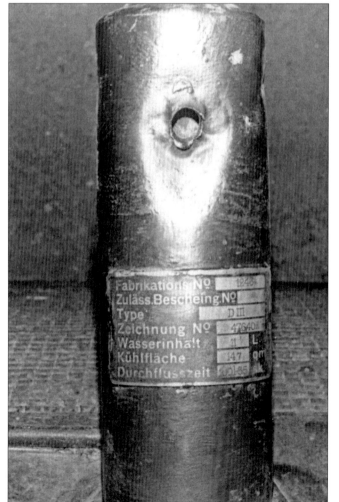

Above: The radiator removed from the upper wing showing the shutters in an open position.

Facing Page: The The restored radiator in November 2023. Note the pipe taking overflow water to the header tank. It has been removed to facilitate storage of the upper wing. The cone gives pressure to the water in the radiator.

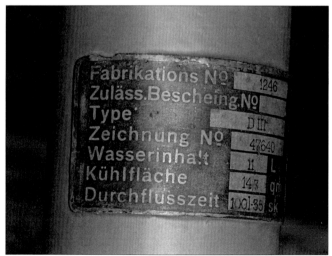

Above: Closeup of the radiator's header tank manufacturer's plate before restoration.

Left: The radiator's header tank before restoration.

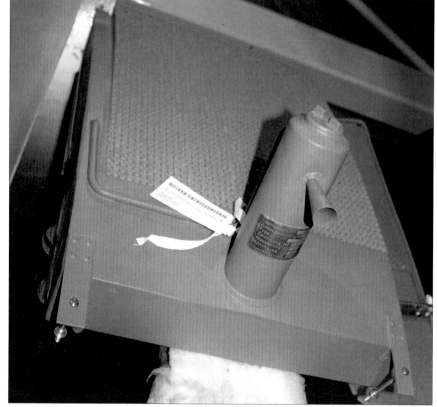

Above & Left: The The restored radiator in November 2023. Note the pipe taking overflow water to the header tank. It has been removed to facilitate storage of the upper wing. The cone gives pressure to the water in the radiator.

Above: View of restored radiator in 2008.

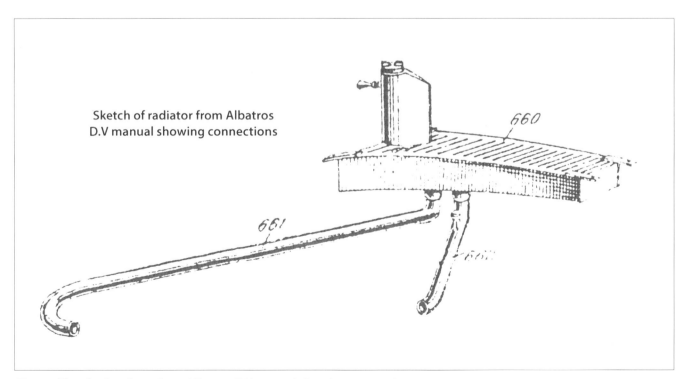

Sketch of radiator from Albatros
D.V manual showing connections

660

661

Above: Sketch of radiator from Albatros D.V manual showing connections.

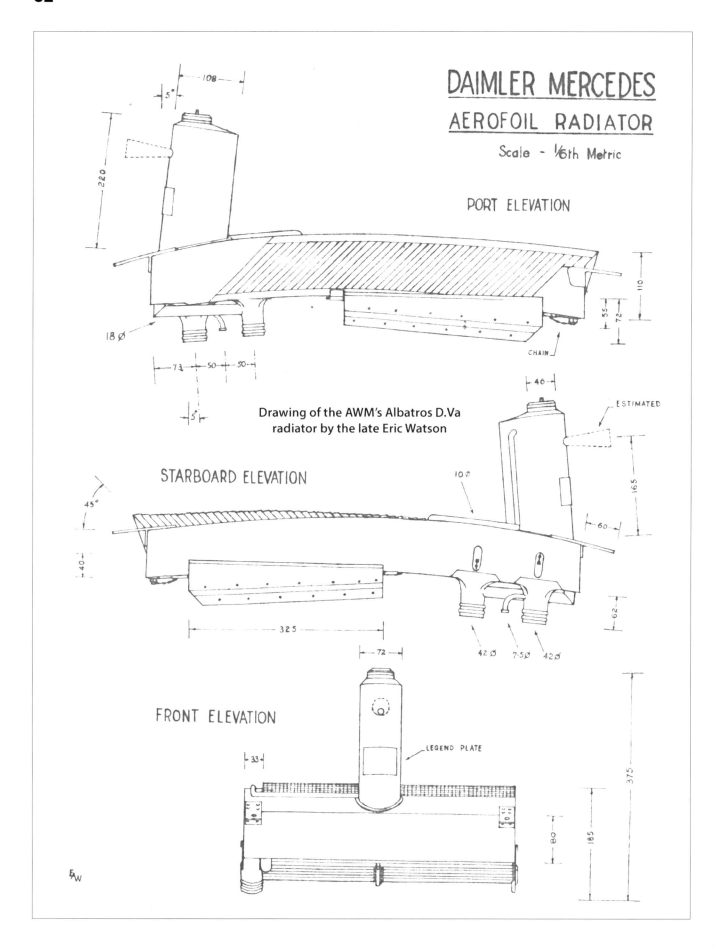

DAIMLER MERCEDES
AEROFOIL RADIATOR
Scale – 1/6th Metric

PORT ELEVATION

108

5°

220

18 Ø

7·3 50 50

5°

CHAIN

55
72
110

Drawing of the AWM's Albatros D.Va
radiator by the late Eric Watson

STARBOARD ELEVATION

45°

40

325

40

ESTIMATED

10 Ø

165

60

62

42 Ø 7·50 42 Ø

72

FRONT ELEVATION

33

LEGEND PLATE

375

185

80

E W

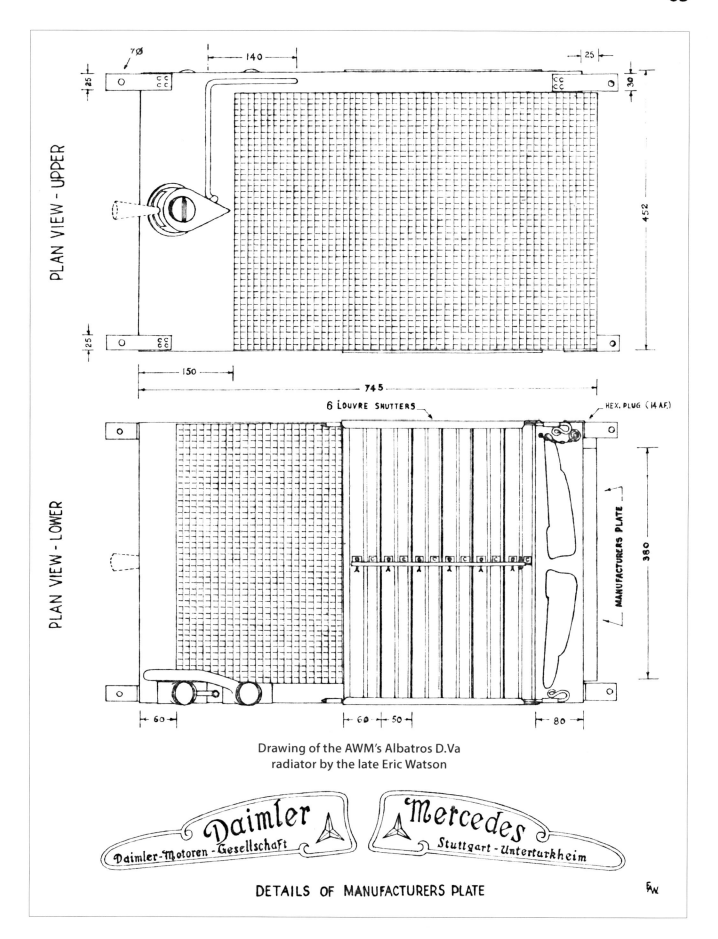

PLAN VIEW - UPPER

PLAN VIEW - LOWER

6 LOUVRE SHUTTERS

HEX. PLUG (14 A.F.)

MANUFACTURERS PLATE

Drawing of the AWM's Albatros D.Va
radiator by the late Eric Watson

DETAILS OF MANUFACTURERS PLATE

The Fuselage

Above & Below: Two views of the fuselage while displayed at the Camden Aviation Museum.

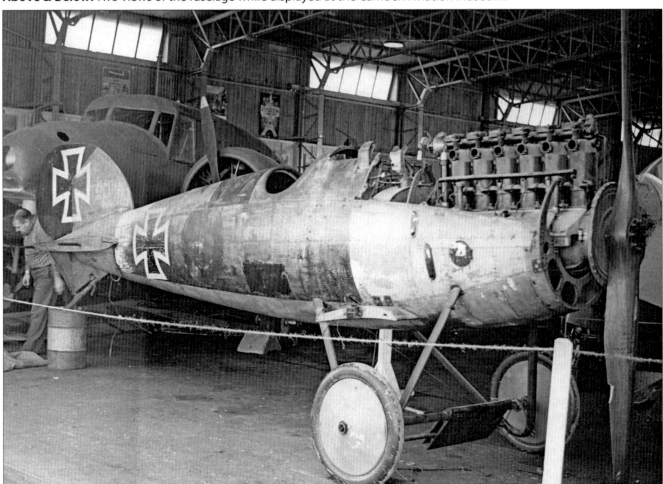

Fuselage Formers			
Former No.	Thickness in mm	Outer ply in mm	Notes
1	15	3	
2	13	1.5	
3	18	3	
4	15	2	
4a	15	2	
5	27	2	
5a	15	2	Has lower wing spar mount.
6	18	2	Has additional support at centre longeron.
6a		1.5	
7	12	1.5	Has additional 1.5 plywood web on front face.
8	13.5	2	
9	11.5	2	
10	11.5		
11			Externally reinforced.
12	12	2	
13	18		Entirely laminated of 2 mm plywood.
Notes: 1. Outer skin is all 3-ply birch plywood. Inner skin is of 3 laminations of Linden pieces. 2. The above information was extracted from material in the NASM.			

The fuselage was constructed of wood around a skeleton framework of three longerons per side supporting 14 ply formers, with steel reinforcing brackets at locations that required strengthening. There are, properly speaking, no internal struts, bracing wires or diagonal members, except where needed in front of the pilot's seat to carry the guns, instruments, etc. The bottom longeron is of ash from the nose to splice then pine. The other two are pine. Former No. 1 forms the front end of the engine bay, and supports the aft end of the lower engine cowl panel. Former No. 14 forms the aft fin post. The rudder is attached to this post. The fuselage is covered with formed birch plywood panels with overlapping edges that form a scarf joint of approx. 50

mm. The panels are 2 mm thick except for 3 mm thick panels around the engine bay. What is not evident from an outside glance at the fuselage is that the scarf joint is not located at the position of the formers as would be expected. The two sides were pre-shaped on wooden forms and then placed onto the fuselage frame and glued in place.[33] The panels are glued and nailed in place to form a robust shell. Hatches introduced into this shell give access to the engine bay, foot step, etc. These are covered with metal hinged doors.

The plywood on either side of the engine on top of a longeron and running aft to Former No. 4 have been replaced with plywood of slightly different finish and quality. This is thought to have been a German wartime repair.

Sketch showing the scarf joint of the fuselage panels. AFT ⟶

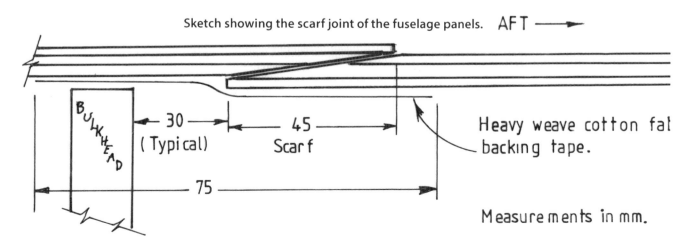

BULKHEAD

← 30 → (Typical)   ← 45 → Scarf

← 75 →

Heavy weave cotton fabric backing tape.

Measurements in mm.

Above: The rear of the fuselage ply at the cockpit had been given this rough repair at some time.

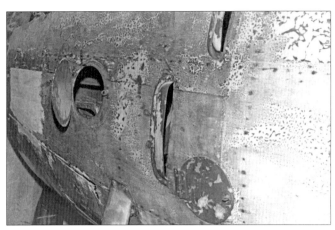

Above & Below Left: Close-up of the front fuselage as delivered to the Camden Aviation Museum.

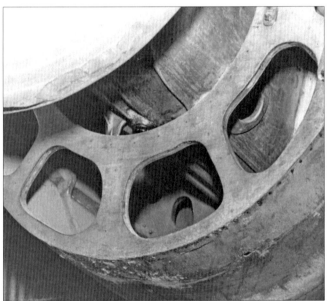

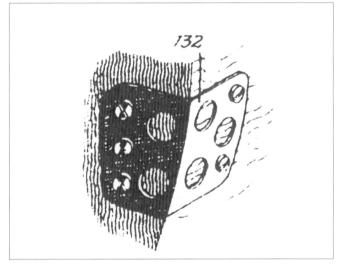

Above: Sketch from Albatros D.V manual showing metal reinforcement fitting at front former.

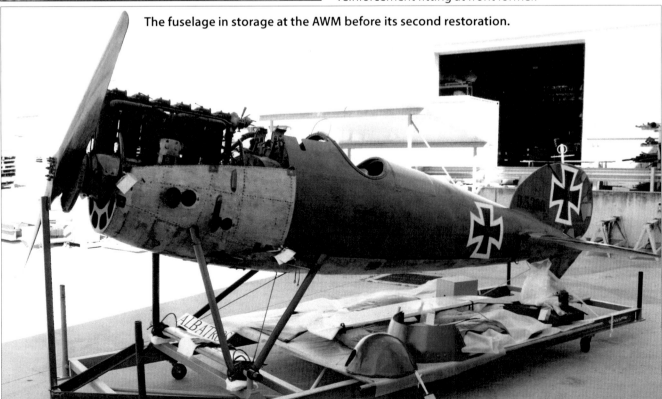

The fuselage in storage at the AWM before its second restoration.

Above: The fuselage in storage at the AWM before its second restoration.

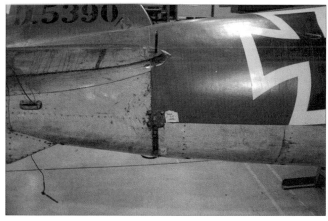

Above, Below, Above Right, Below Right: The fuselage in its rotating frame showing details of metal fittings, damage and AWM notes for restoration

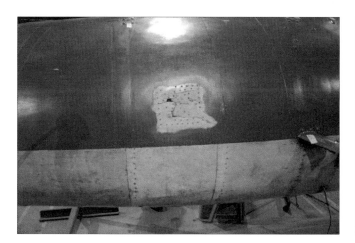

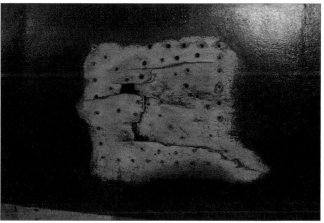

Above: The fuselage in its rotating frame showing details of metal fittings, damage and AWM notes for restoration

Above & Below Left: Detail over rear fuselage showing painting sequence determined by careful sanding back of paint coats.

Below & Below Right: Details of the support strap and lifting handles.

Detail of elevator cable access to fuselage.

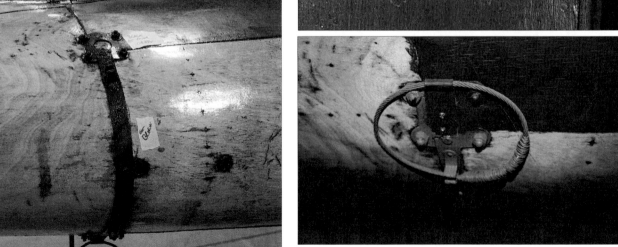

Above, Above Left, & Below Left: Details of the stub wing.

Below: View of bottom of fuselage showing access doors and oil staining to fuselage. The smaller inspection door (166 mm diameter) has a hole for drainage. Note also the drainage holes in the lower stub wings.

Above: Access door on the fuselage side. All access doors are slightly bulged to conform to the shape of the fuselage.

Above: The louvre to the engine bay has been removed showing nail holes that hold it in place.

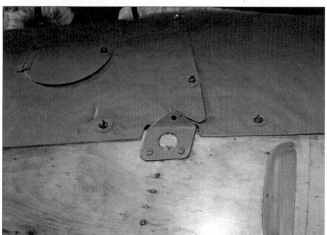

Above, Lrft, Facing Page, Following Page Above: Details on the restored fuselage. The metal work has been restored and repainted. 2023 photograph.

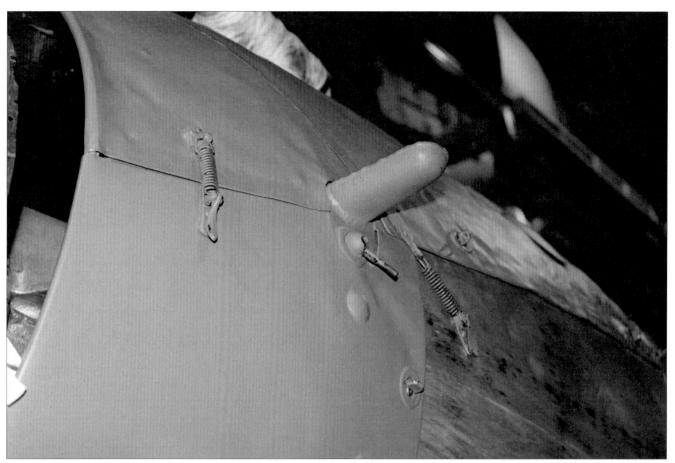

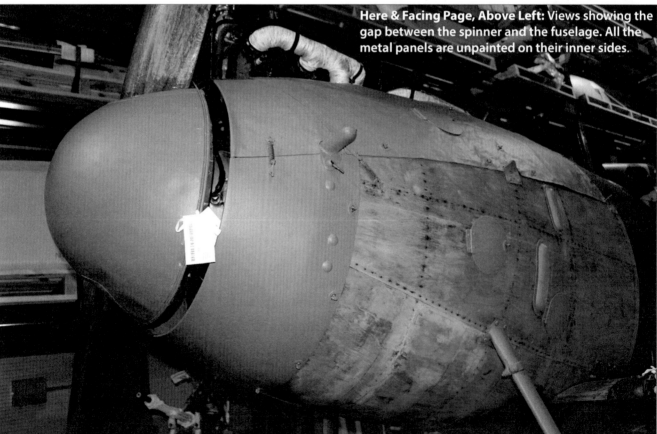

Here & Facing Page, Above Left: Views showing the gap between the spinner and the fuselage. All the metal panels are unpainted on their inner sides.

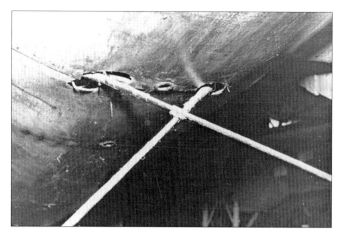

Above: The undercarriage bracing wires showing damage when at the Camden Aviation Museum. Note the drain hole between the two wires.

Above: Moving forward to drainage door under engine. Note drain hole and damage to fuselage.

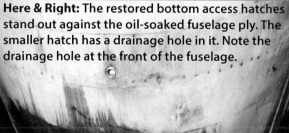

Here & Right: The restored bottom access hatches stand out against the oil-soaked fuselage ply. The smaller hatch has a drainage hole in it. Note the drainage hole at the front of the fuselage.

Albatros D.Va D.5253/17 of the first batch was captured after being brought down by AA fire on 14 November 1917. It is shown at the Agricultural Hall at Islington with its fuselage stripped to show the internal structure. The positions of the formers and longerons are well shown. This machine had Fokker synchronising gear fitted. The wheel covers were of ply. (H. Woodman collection via R. Rimell)

The fuselage suspended in the rotating frame.

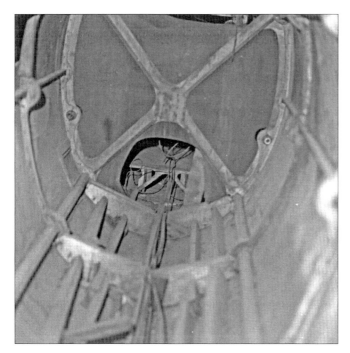

Above: View of Former 8 looking aft. Note the fabric behind the former. Photographs taken at Camden Aviation Museum.

Right: The fuselage in the rotating frame. Former 8 looking aft. The seat supports are well shown.

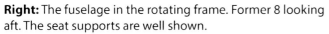
Note the dirt, dust, and material that has accumulated in the fuselage over 50 years.

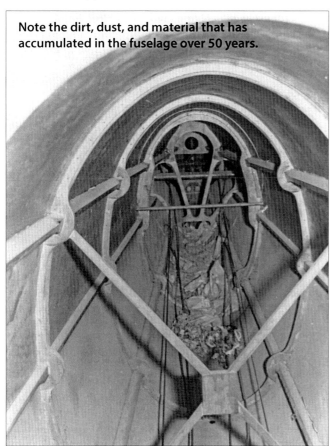

View showing fin and rudder support.

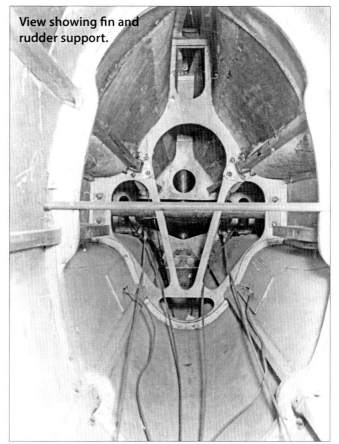

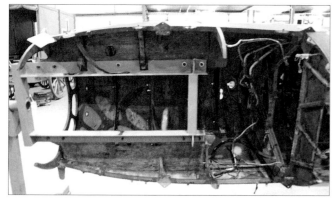

Above: View showing the support bolted to the engine bearers. The area behind the engine contained the fuel tanks, then the ammunition boxes. The remnants of the original electrical wiring, engine piping, control rods, etc., may be seen.

Above & Below: Views of the engine bearers showing the clips for holding the engine cowling in place and metal attachment for the drift cable.

The original internal finish was mainly a light grey-green German primer paint, although some surfaces were varnished.

The lower wing fillets are formed into the plywood fuselage structure. Two additional part formers reinforce this area.

Two heavy timber engine bearers are supported by

Above: View from the front looking at the cockpit section. Note the machine gun supports.

Above: View showing the support bolted to the engine bearers. The area behind the engine contained the fuel tanks, then the ammunition boxes. The remnants of the original electrical wiring, engine piping, control rods, etc., may be seen.

Formers Nos. 1 to 4.

Steel angle brackets on the upper parts of formers No. 3 and 5 provide attachment points for the struts that support the upper wing. These struts were formed from three lengths of aerofoil shaped steel tube assembled into an N shape, with welded attachment brackets at top and bottom.

Body filler had been used in the 1960's work and this had to be removed. There were dents in the fuselage, no doubt caused by its use and handling over 100 years.

The lower half of the fuselage insides was grey from the accumulated dust and dirt. A repair to the top of the fuselage behind the cockpit had bevelled edges. This was nailed in place with the nails protruding to the inside of the skin.

The underside around the water tank and sump access was stained by oil leaking from the engine.

Extensive cracking was visible in the panels between the

Above, Left, & Facing Page, Below Righ: The area immediately behind the engine bearers showing Former 5 with the machine gun mounts.

Above: The auxiliary and fuel tank.

Above: Auxiliary fuel tank.

Above: The auxiliary fuel tank.

View of cockpit area showing the rudder bar.

undercarriage and forward of the undercarriage struts.

Many of the internal frames were cracked and damaged.

The rear of the fuselage that tapers to a horizontal knife edge for the elevator, is sound.

The front cowl panel is made of soft sheet aluminium whose internal surface was unpainted. The edges are rolled and flattened to provide reinforcement, with the addition of a reinforcing wire inside the fold on the top edge.

Endnote

1. The research done for the NASM Albatros restoration noted that *since many of the cloth tapes* (at the scarfed joint) *are sandwiched between the bulkheads and skin, it seems the skin was laid up and glued in molds, and then glued onto the framework.* (NASM notes via late R. Waugh). However, photographs from the Oeffag works show the Albatros skin on wooden forms See *WWI Aero* No. 128. P.44. For photographs of the NASM's forming of the fuselage panels for their rebuild, see Mikesh, R.C. *Albatros D.Va German Fighter of World War I*, Smithsonian Institution Press, USA, 1980.

Albatros D.Va 5390/17
Ltn.d.R. **Rudolf Clauss**
Jasta **29**
December 1917
As captured

Engine, Propeller, and Armament

Above & Above Right: As can be seen, the engine panels and spinner were in a bad condition when the aircraft was delivered to the Camden Aviation Museum.

Above, Left, & Below: These views show the wrong engine installed in the Albatros when it was delivered to the Camden Aviation Museum.

The engine has dual throttle control, one by rod on the side of the fuselage and the other by Bowden wire from the control stick.

The fuel tanks are located immediately at the rear of the engine and are constructed of brass sheet with four small manufacturers labels on the top of the tank. The emergency tank is located directly on top of the main tank. Its filler tube passing through the emergency tank. Two brass caps, one marked BENZINE are on the top of the tank. The British report gave the capacity as 22 gallons.[34]

Above: The Albatros on display at Camden with the engine panels removed.

Above: View of engine installed May 2021.

The oil tank is located on the right side of the engine. It was assessed as carrying 2 gallons.[35]

The two original Maxim LMG 08/15 machine guns are mounted on the fuselage in front of the pilot. They have no breech blocks. The ammunition bins are incomplete with part of the chutes missing.

Above: View from the cockpit. Note the ammunition chutes in front of the engine.

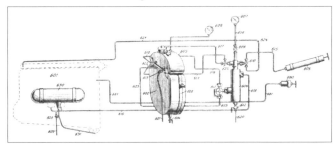

Above: Sketch from the Albatros D.V manual showing the fuel system. No. 605 is the Air Pressure Pump. No. 680 is the Grease Gun for the water pump. No. 602 is the main fuel tank, with No. 603, the gravity tank, sitting on top.

The large, curved exhaust manifold is fabricated from steel tube and fits all six cylinders of a Mercedes engine. This item appears to be an original as it is of German manufacture and matches that fitted when photographs were taken of the machine after capture. The notes from the Camden Museum restoration state that a reproduction exhaust pipe was constructed by the RAAF for the machine. It would appear that this was replaced by an original German when back in the AWM's hands.

Above: The spinner suffered through its years of display until the 1960s restoration.

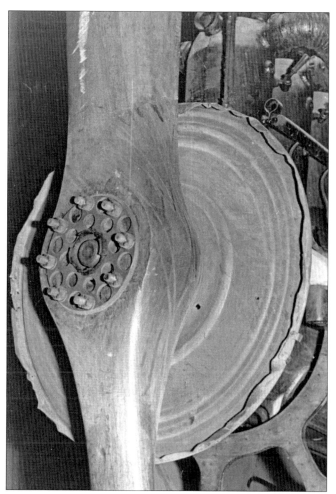

Above & Above Right: The original airscrew had been replaced sometime by another. The backing plate for the spinner is well shown here.

Right: View of the machine when presented after its 2008 restoration. The stands are used so that less stress is placed on the undercarriage.

Above & Above Right: The ammunition boxes that carry the belts and feed the machine guns.

Right: The box that takes the belts after firing. The box is made of soft thin aluminium, 0.020 inch thick.

Propeller

The airscrew fitted is not that it had at the time of capture. A receipt, dated 25 May 1918, in the British Log Book confirms that the original airscrew No. 16969 was on the aircraft when it was dismantled for shipment to Australia. The airscrew fitted to the machine must have been replaced after the aircraft arrived in Australia.

Spinner

The spinner is made from sheet aluminium. *Bob* Waugh recorded that it was painted chocolate brown. The internal surface is unpainted.[36]

The edges of the spinner are rolled back to form a channel that holds a cable used to clamp the spinner to the backing plate. Where the airscrew fits in the two cut-outs, the spinner is reinforced on the internal surface by a riveted steel plate.

The spinner's backing plate is made from stamped aluminium. The edge was shaped to form a channel that fits in a corresponding one on the spinner and allows the cable to hold the spinner in place. This was fitted back to front during the 1960s restoration.

Endnotes

1. Report on Albatros G.101. TNA AIR1/1193/204/5.
2. *Ibid.*
3. The author has to admit that Bob had sent him a tiny sample of this colour, but to his shame, he lost it.

Above: View of the restored ammunition boxes.

Above: This view shows the restored seat, ammunition boxes and the box for the belts.

Above: Detail of the feed at the top of the ammunition box. 2023 photograph.

Above: The machine guns are missing in this view of the machine before its first restoration The feeds to the guns may be seen.

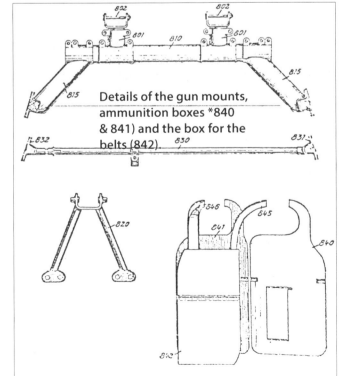

Details of the gun mounts, ammunition boxes *840 & 841) and the box for the belts (842).

Above: The rear of the gun mounts with the fuel tank filler pipes behind.

Above & Below: Views of the mounted machine guns.

The Cockpit

Above: View of the cockpit before restoration.

Above: The original windscreen when removed from the aircraft at the Camden Aviation Museum. The mounting is made of aluminium with the transparent section held by soft aluminium rivets.

The pilot position was just behind the trailing edge of the top wing that was cut out at its centre to improve his upward vision.

The windscreen is mounted in front of the pilot. The frame is aluminium.

There is no evidence that an ASI was ever fitted in the cockpit or on the port outer wing strut.

The pilot's seat is adjustable being mounted on two tubes on each side of the fuselage. It may be moved forward and backwards on the rails. The seat has cracks in the wood at its base. The seat retains its original back upholstery, largely intact except for a 130 mm vertical slit that was repaired. The seat with its rails assembly is mounted at Former No. 6 and runs back to Former No. 7.

Right: The ammunition box in front of the rear bar that carries the machine guns. Note the instrument panel to starboard.

Above: This view shows the relationship of the engine, machine gun mounts, and cockpit with the starboard side instruments shown.

Above: View of the Albatros after its first restoration showing the handle from the radiator and machine guns installed.

Above: The RPM gauge is carried on the cross bar that supports the machine gun mounts. The original William Morell gauge was missing when the Albatros was handed over to the AWM and this original German one (s/n 58164) was purchased in 1997.

 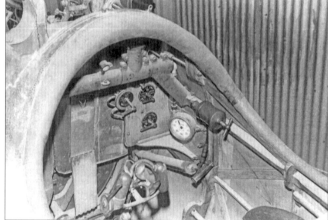

Above & Above Right: The starboard side of the cockpit showing the hand pump and the fuel-air control dashboard.

Above & Above Right: The starboard side of the cockpit showing the hand pump and the fuel-air control dashboard.

Above: View of the restored cockpit in 2023 showing the hand pump.

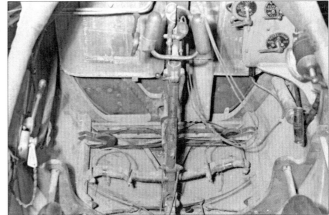

Above & Above Right: These views This view shows the control column. Each machine gun could be fired separately or together. The large aluminium box to the left is the box that receives the spent ammunition belts. shows the control column. Each machine gun could be fired separately or together. The large aluminium box to the left is the box that receives the spent ammunition belts.

Above: Bottom of the control column showing the rudder bar and compass. There was no compass fitted when the machine was passed over to the AWM, and this original German compass (s/n 19418) was purchased in 1997 for installation in the airframe. Note the seat rail on the right.

Above, Below Left, & Below: Detail views of the controls.

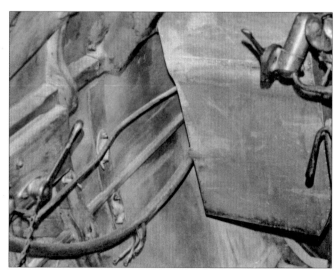

Above & Above Right: The View of the starboard side of the cockpit before and after restoration, showing the ammunition belt box

Above: Detail view of magneto key switch and spark control handle. before restoration.

Above: The Bosch starter magneto was missing and a replacement one was fitted during the 2008 restoration. fitted.

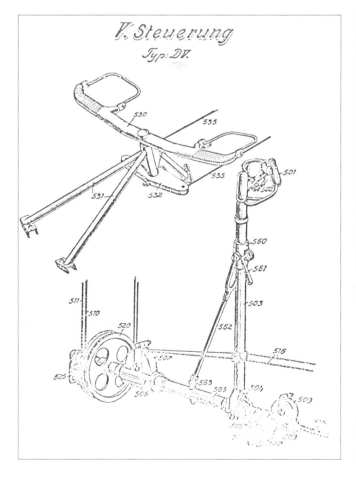

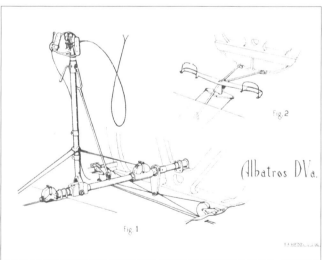

Above: Sketch of the AWM's D.Va controls by the late Eric Watson.

Left: Sketch of the controls from the Albatros D.V manual. The aileron controls were the only visible change from the D.V to the D.Va.

Above: The seat in position in the cockpit before restoration.

Above & Right: Views of the pilot's seat.

Above: Detail of seat support. Note safety belt over steel tube.

Above: Detail of the pilot's safety harness.

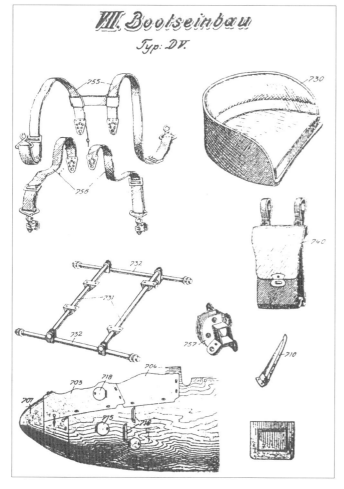

Above: Sketch of the seat and fittings from the Albatros D.V manual.

The Tailplane, Fin & Rudder

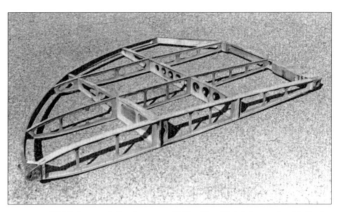

Above, Right, & Below: The stripped tailplane showing construction at Camden. Note the three holes for aligning the tailplane to the fuselage.

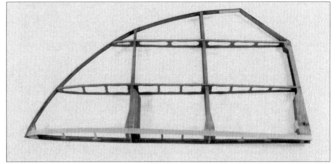

Above: The stripped tailplane in the AWM for restoration and covering with correct fabric.

Above: The tailplane in the process of covering at the AWM.

Above: Detail of the wooden construction of the tailplane.

The Horizontal Tailplane

The fixed horizontal tailplane is constructed of wood around two veneer timber spars with metal brackets and fitting. It was covered with fabric. The leading edge is a milled half-round section. The tailplane is connected to the fuselage by a bolt at the leading edge and by two tubes, one at the forward spar and the other at the trailing edge. The elevator is attached to the rear spar by two attachments on each half of the tailplane. These attachments were steel strips folded into a U shape and secured by a bolt.

Some splitting of the timber on the port tailplane had occurred near the mount socket. On the starboard side there were damaged timber on four webs.

The Elevator

The single piece elevator is formed of welded steel tube with a number of timber pieces. The framing follows the rib positioning of the tailplane. The four hinge straps are held in place by profiled timber blocks. Missing hinges and hinge blocks were replaced.

The Fin

The fin is integral with the fuselage being supported by Formers Nos. 12 to 14. The sides of these formers are flat

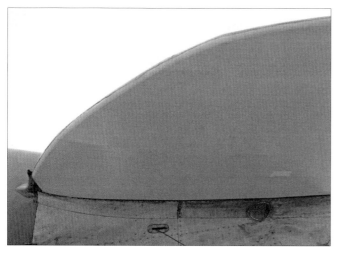 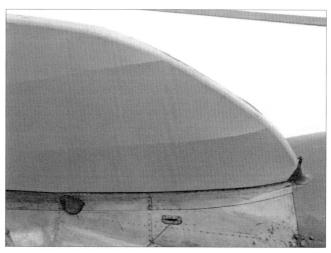

Above, Above Right, & Below: The tailplane before restoration. Note the small metal fixture at the front of the tailplane where it joins the fuselage.

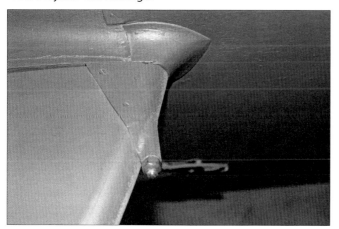 

Above: View of the fuselage showing the tailplane mounded into the fuselage and the tailplane connectors.

Above & Above Right: The horizontal tailplane is attached to the fuselage by the three attachment points starting at the front, then centre and rear.

to which are attached the horizontal tailplanes by two horizontal tubes located at Formers Nos. 12 and 13 and the horizontal stern post respectively. The horizontal knife edge trailing edge of the fuselage is concave to allow for the fitting of the one-piece elevator.

The Rudder

The balanced rudder is constructed of welded steel tube and covered in fabric. When it left the factory, the rudder was covered with lozenge fabric. Four timber blocks are attached to the leading edge for the attachment of the hinge straps. The rudder controls are contained within the fuselage.

A cross of smaller proportions to that overpainted was visible under the existing cross.

Right: Sketch from the Albatros D.V manual showing tailplane, rudde, and elevator details.

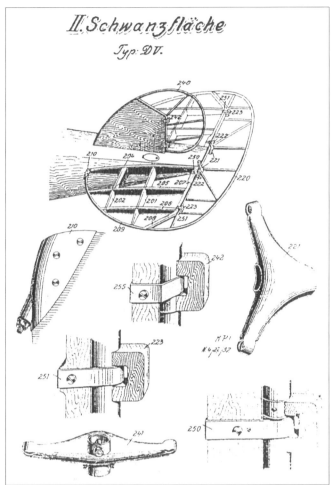

Above: The elevator when delivered to Camden Air Museum.

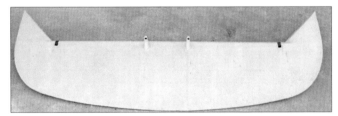

Above: The Camden restoration of the elevator. Note the control horns and the attachment points for the hinges.

Right: The elevator control wires connected to the elevator horns. Note the elevator hinges, a steel strap wound round the elevator spar. Photograph taken before any restoration effort.

Above: The stripped elevator showing the welded steel tube construction.

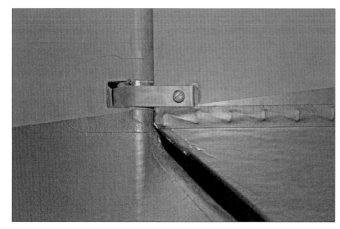

Above: The stripped elevator showing the welded steel tube construction.

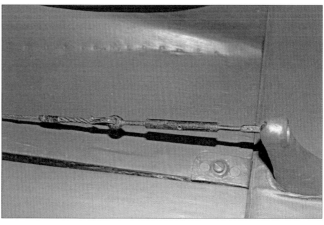

Above, Below, Below Left: Detail of upper surface elevator control wires.

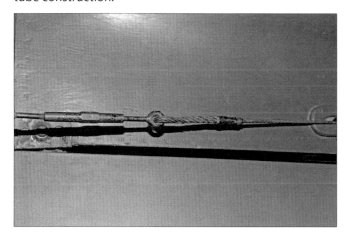

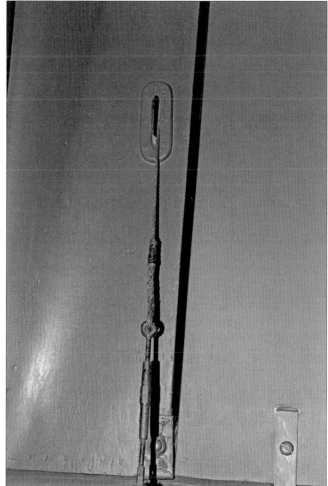

Above: Lower surface elevator wires pass into the side of the fuselage.

Above: Rear view of fuselage showing the tailplane attachment pipes and the elevator cut away.

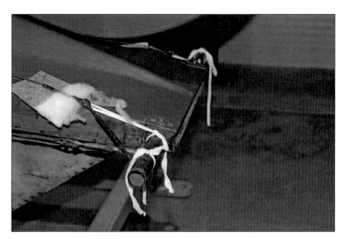

Above: View of the rear tube attachment point for tailplane.

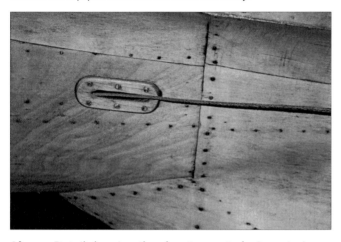

Above: Detail showing the elevator control wire entering fuselage here.

Above: The stripped rudder showing its welded metal tube construction. Note wooden blocks at hinge locations to support fabric there.

Above: The rudder on arrival at Camden Aviation Museum. The flaking of the paint on the fuselage is well shown here. This original fabric had apparently gone missing during the first restoration.

Right: The restored rudder was covered with plain fabric. 13 April 2008.

Below: The restored rudder on the fuselage. 20 May 2021.

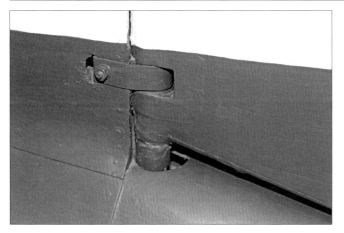

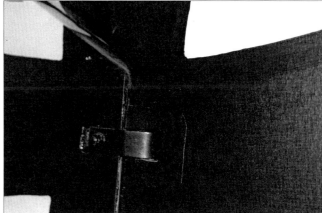

Above & Above Right: Details of the rudder hinges. 20 May 2021.

The Undercarriage

Above: This photograph shows the undercarriage as delivered to the Camden Aviation Museum.

Above: The Restored undercarriage in 2023.

Above, Right, Facing Page Above: More views of the unrestored undercarriage. The struts are braced by a horizontal steel tube that runs through this fairing. Note the lack of shock absorbers. The fairing has three hinges on the leading edge. The rear is held in place by two springs at the trailing edge. The fairing was in bad condition even after the first restoration.

The tyres have been replaced with wooden reproductions. The original plywood wheel covers have been replaced with galvanised metal reproductions.

The undercarriage struts are of aerofoil section steel tube. Brackets to attach the vee-type undercarriage legs are fitted to the lower part of formers Nos. 4 and 6. The struts are braced by a horizontal steel tube that runs through the fairing and it attached to each strut by a bolt at the axle position. The struts are also cross braced by wires.

The axle fairing is of aerofoil shape and constructed in two sections joined at the leading edge by three hinges and secured by two springs at the trailing edge.

The upper and lower surfaces have suffered from oil leaking from the motor.

The tail skid is anchored to formers Nos. 13 and 14 and faired into the fuselage by a plywood fin. The tail skid is hinged by a bracket supported by and at the rear end of the under fin. The forward end is supported by the bound shock absorber cord that passes through a slot cut in the fin. The fin acts as a streamline for the front end of the skid.

The tail skid's rubber shock absorber was missing although the wrapping marks were visible.

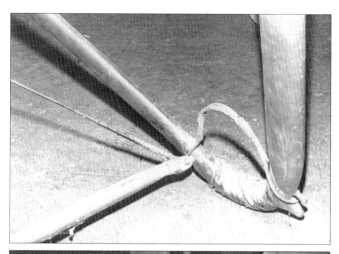

Above, Right, Following Page Above: The missing shock absorber has been replaced by wrapped rubber cord. The white material is to prevent movement in storage. The bracing tube's connection to the rear leg of the undercarriage V-strut is formed by the ends of the tube being flattened and welded and drilled to give a tab that is bolted to the undercarriage leg. Note also the cross-bracing wire's attachment to the bracing tube. Also noteworthy is the back-up restraining wire, with the hooks on the landing gear to hold it in place, if the bungee cord gave way.

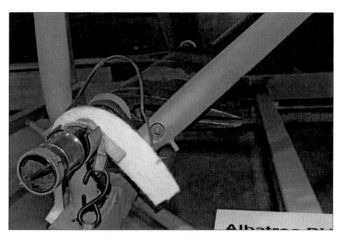

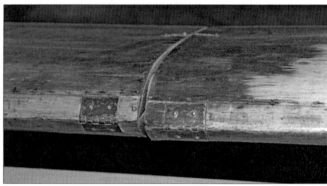

Above: The ply axle cover during the 2008 restoration. Note the cross-bracing cables on the undercarriage legs.

Above: Close-up of the central join in the aerofoil shaped ply axle covering. 2023.

Above & Facing Page, Above: The restored fuselage in storage 2023 showing the undercarriage to fuselage attachments.

Above: View showing the axle, shock absorber safety strap and aerofoil covering to the axle. The damage caused by leaking oil is well shown here.

Above & Above Right: These photographs were taken of the undercarriage bracket when the fuselage was suspended in the rotating frame. The stub wing has the rear edge routed to allow for the undercarriage leg.

Above: View of the rear undercarriage strut bracket that was attached to the forward face of Former No. 6.

Above: View with the strut in place before restoration.

Above: View with the strut in place after restoration.

Above, Left, & Below Left: Views of the rear fuselage area around the tailskid at the Camden Aviation Museum before the first restoration. Points to note are the elevator control entry into the fuselage; lifting handle and associated strap; the shock absorber has been lost and wire used to maintain the skid in position.

Below: With the fuselage in the rotating frame the under fin could be examined for the tailskid attachments. Note the open hatch for checking the rudder cables.

Above & Below: With the fuselage in the rotating frame the under fin could be examined for the tailskid attachments. Note the open hatch for checking the rudder cables.

Above: View of the tail skid to fuselage connection from underneath showing the elevator cables and fuselage drain hole.

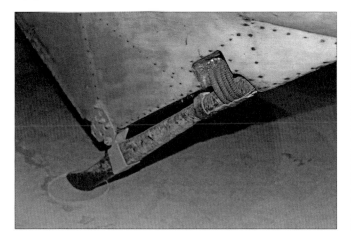

Above & Above Right: The restored tailskid when displayed in the 'Over the Front' exhibition.

Above: View of tailskid and tailplane connection while machine is in storage. 2023.

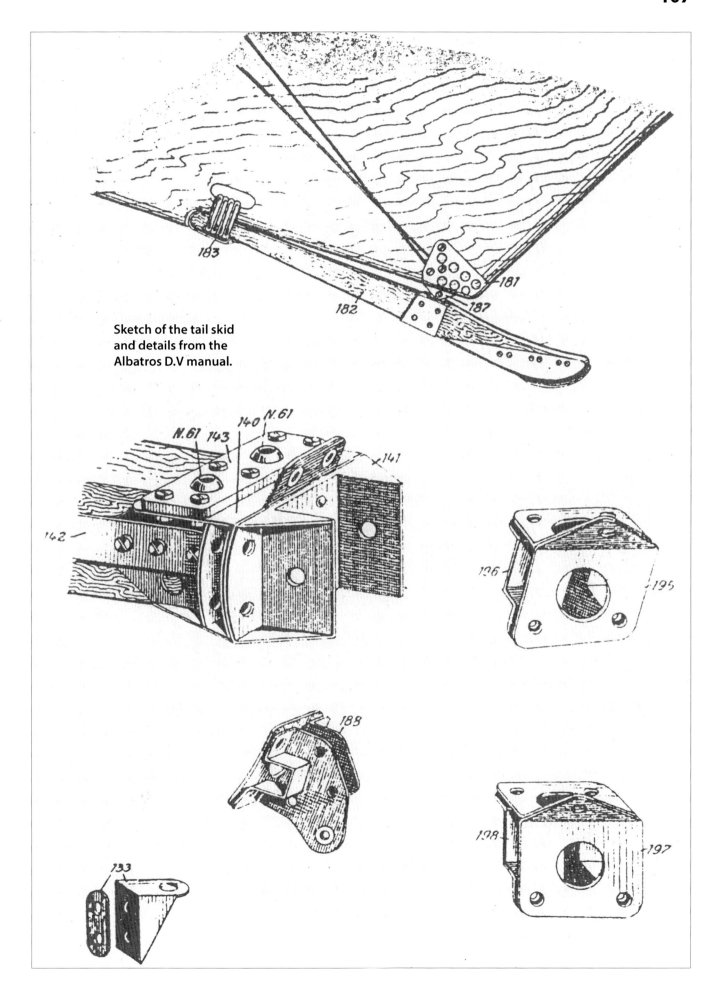

Sketch of the tail skid
and details from the
Albatros D.V manual.

Colours and Markings

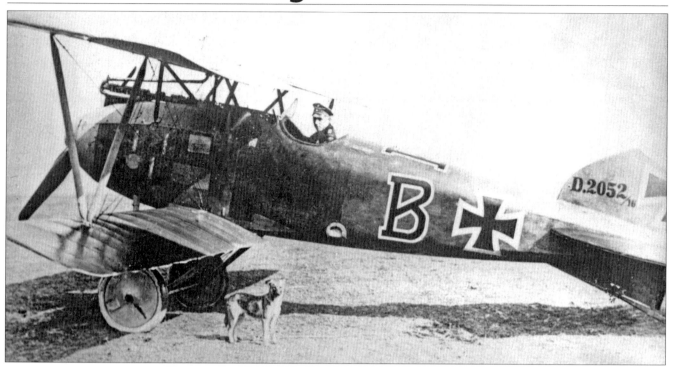

Above: *Ltn*. Hans Hermann von Budde in his Albatros D.III, before the introduction of the drak green fuselage marking. (via Greg VanWyngarden)

Above: A *Jasta* 29 Albatros D.Va, with a personal emblem of an eagle on its dark green fuselage (via Greg VanWyngarden)

Above: This *Jasta* 29 Albatros D.Va served as a backdrop for a funeral. The dark green fuselage and yellow nose are evident. (via Greg VanWyngarden)

Perhaps the most controversial aspect of the restoration and conservations of D.5390/17 has been its colour schemes. The machine had been repaired and worked on without any documentation being kept so that it has been necessary to consult the photographs taken of the machine when recovered by the AFC before it went into British hands and the process of repainting began. It is thought that the weight's legend was overpainted and after the aircraft's capture the overpainting was scrapped off.

The aircraft had the standard German green and mauve upper surface colours. It had been constructed at the time the pre-printed five-colour fabric was coming into use, and although the wings were mainly covered with lozenge fabric, they were over sprayed with coloured dope on their upper surfaces. The horizontal tailplane was finished the same way. The lower planes were sprayed light blue except that the upper wing's undersurface was left as doped and varnished lozenge fabric.

In service the fuselage, including the cross, was over painted green. An original paint sample was found on the starboard side of the fuselage near the cockpit. The metal panels were a grey-green colour. From the photographs taken at No. 3 Squadron's aerodrome immediately after capture it is evident that the tailplane has been overpainted. Bob Waugh noted the tailplane and elevator was green and light blue with the light blue in the centre of the tailplane.[37]

The machine was given British cockades and the British serial G.101. When it was placed on display at Australia House, its British markings were replaced/overpainted and it was given German type crosses, with one being added to the fuselage.

In 1927 a report recommended that the Albatros and Pfalz be given an overall one colour finish. The Memorial staff replied that *as they are the only known examples of practical camouflage of this nature we possess* this would be a detrimental decision. It is not known what was done, but the upper wing and tailplane of the Albatros had been repainted a dark green colour previously, probably British dope.[38]

Robert *Bob* Waugh had examined the Albatros when on display in the AWM and Eric Watson had taken notes of it during its restoration at Camden. They stated that the upper surface of both wing was dark green and mauve camouflage

Above: *Ltn*. Eugen Siempelkamp of *Jasta* 29 and his Pfalz with green fuselage, yellow nose and black stripes on the underside.

Ltn. Siempelkamp of *Jasta* 29 in his Pfalz with its dark green fuselage, yellow nose and black stripes on the bottom.

Above: *Vzfw*. Karl Pech of *Jasta* 29 with his dark green Pfalz D.IIIa, with yellow nose.

All photos these two pages via Greg VanWyngarden.

Right: This *Jasta* 29 Albatros fuselage displays the dark green finish with yellow nose, and black stripes underneath

applied over the standard lozenge fabric. The sprayed colours had a hard edge between the two colours about 10-15 mm wide rather than a blended sprayed edge.

The colour scheme that the Albatros wore when it was returned to the AWM after the 1960s 'restoration' was not that it wore when captured. *The drab charcoal finish on the aeroplanes when brought to Camden was not the original factory finish*, and the Camden Museum of Aviation staff recommended to the AWM that it be restored to the original factory standard. The AWM accepted the proposed changes. *Restoration colours were selected from the evidence revealed in studies during the stripping of parts.*[39] The advice of *Bob* Waugh and others was ignored.

For the 2008 conservation the remains of the original fabric were obtained from the Camden Museum of Aviation and closely examined to determine the colours and position of the fabric enabling it to be replaced as close to the original as possible.

The underside of the upper wing was in the light five-colour lozenge fabric. The starboard aileron was lozenge pattern overall, most probably replacement item. The aircraft's number was applied in white paint to the starboard aileron. The interplane struts were light grey while the cabane and undercarriage struts were khaki. The spinner and metal panels were dark brown. The rudder was dark green, same as fuselage, over lozenge fabric. The lower surfaces of the fuselage were left as factory finish of varnished wood. The German cross on the fuselage had been overpainted but could be seen through the paint. The serial number was in black over varnished wood on the port side of the fin only. A weights legend stencil was caried on the fuselage. The serial number was applied to both sides of the fin in black paint. It is only faintly visible in photographs taken at the time of its capture, however it was noted by No. 3 Squadron at that time and may have been thinly overpainted with the green colour.[40]

Wheel hubs were grey.

The upper wing was trimmed with 30 mm tapes on the leading and trailing edges. These are light purple in colour.

Metal fittings such as the radiator and strut attachment brackets were painted in grey-green finish.

In order to replicate the method of applying the fabric to a 1914-1918 aircraft, the Memorial arranged for a special team of French experts to come to Canberra and apply the replica lozenge pre-printed fabric to the Albatros and Pfalz D.XII.[41] The gaining of access to substantial amounts of original fabric from the 1960s restoration, with the exception of the rudder and ailerons, enabled significant analysis of the fabric to be undertaken.

The lozenge fabric on the undersurface of the top wing has the seam running spanwise as the fabric was applied spanwise rather than chord wise.

Lavender coloured tapes for ribs, etc., appear to have been mechanically produced in widths of 20 mm and 30 mm. The radiator has 7 mm tapes surrounding it.[42]

End Notes:

1. It has been stated in some references that part of the fin on the port was left unpainted to show the serial number (Nemles, M. P.31), however the photographs that appear to show this were taken after the machine came into British hands. No photographs of the port side taken at the time the machine was on No. 3's airfield appear to have survived, if indeed, they were ever taken.

2. The Pfalz D.XII's upper surface of the top wing was also overpainted dark green. It has not been possible to ascertain when the overpainting was carried out.

3. Lalas, H. 'The 1966 Restoration of Albatros D.Va' (as told by Harold and Alan Thomas in 1995). *Aviation Heritage*. June 2015. P.82. Unfortunately, there seems to be no record that this evidence of colours was kept.

4. It was common practice for German units to overpaint their aircraft, however, weight was always a concern and the colours were always thinly applied and, on many photographs, the original markings may be discerned through the overpaint.

5. Harris, L. *'Naked Birds' Land at Memorial*. 28.02.2008. AWM Blog Archive. See also Dunnell, B. 'Living Memory.' (*Aeroplane*, UK. September 2023. P.14.) for an overview of the French Memorial Flight.

6. Pearce, A. 'Albatros Fabric Research." 11.04.2008. AWM Blog Archives.

Above: The original serial exposed by sanding away the green overpainting of the fuselage.

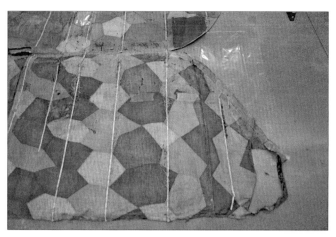

Above: The tapes on the original fabric show the location of the ribs enabling the restoration to accurately replicate the original finish.

Above: The upper wing fabric at the radiator location.

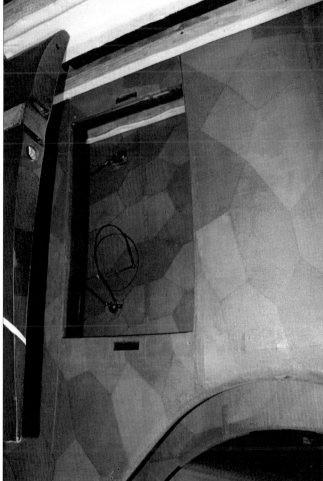

Above: Close-up of the upper wing in storage in 2023 showing the radiator cut out.

Above: The starboard wing's original fabric showing that it was covered in plain fabric.

Above & Above Right: The author and the AWM's John White examining the Memorial's lozenge fabric collection in April 2008. The Albatros D.Va and Pfalz D.XII fuselages are in the background being prepared for restoration for the 'Over the Front' exhibition.

Above & Above Right: The Matching the colours of the new lozenge to original specimens.

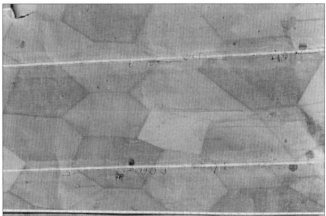

Above: The colours have deteriorated over time and the effect of dope, however the new fabric has been rolled with the original type dyes and is a remarkably close match.

Above: A well-preserved piece of five coloured lozenge in the AWM's collection for colour comparison.

Albatros D.Va 5390/17
As built

Albatros D.Va 5390/17
Ltn.d.R. **Rudolf Clauss**
Jasta **29**
December 1917

Albatros D.Va 5390/17 (G.101)
After capture
December 1917

Afterword: What British Pilots Thought of the Albatros D.Va

Gerald W. Gatherwood undertook experimental test flying while at Martlesham. He flew Albatros D.II D.473/16 at Martlesham on the 13 July 1917, noting that it was *very nice to fly and land.* Albatros D.V (D.2129/17) British No. G.56 was at Martlesham during August–September 1917. Gatherwood found this machine *not as pleasant as the older pattern B. u type. Nose heavy, draughty in cockpit.*[1] Looping the D.V he found that *she tried to fall out sideways.* When he flew Pfalz D.III (D.4184/17) British No. G.141 in March 1918, he recorded that it was *Not so nice as a Vee-strutter.*[2]

Cecil Lewis began his flying career in the cockpit of a Murice Farman Longhorn before his 18th birthday. He flew a variety of aircraft during the war and recounted his experiences in his classic book *Sagittarius Rising.* (Peter Davies, London, 1936).[3] He flew the Sopwith Pup and Camel, and S.E.5a fighters and *a nice red Albatros* that was delivered to the squadron and the pilots were encouraged to take it up after having painted out the German markings and overpainted British roundels.

The monocoque construction of the Albatros *was far in advance of us,* and the engine was big and heavy with a neat radiator in the centre-section. However, he considered that the *machine was sluggish, strong, reliable and determined. It had none of the lightness and grace that our aircraft had. Of course, every aeroplane has its own characteristics and very few pilots could take over the controls of a strange type and really measure up its capabilities in an hour or so. So it is probable that we never really stretched it; but I am certain of one thing – throw an Albatros about in the air was hard work and it would make you sweat in a dogfight.*[4]

The unsigned British report on G.101 found the machine to have very good ease of starting.

The view from the cockpit was very good, *but machine is too slow on controls to manoeuvre.*

There was far too little lateral control. The *Machine can be stunted but with difficulty owing to its general heaviness and sluggishness.*

G.101 was considered unstable longitudinally. Controllability was poor longitudinally as it was *heavy to pull out of a dive,* and also poor laterally as it was *very heavy.* Directionally controllability was good.

It took 100 yards to unstick in a dead calm, and 130 yards to pull up with the engine stopped.

On the ground controllability was considered only fair as the rudder was not coupled to the tail skid.

The controls were well placed. Either of the two synchronised machine guns could be fired separately or both together. The engine controls, magnetos, tanks, controls and cables, etc., were conveniently placed and accessible.[5]

After WWII many of the aircraft that were to be kept for the AWM were disposed of and some were destroyed. The WWI machines were kept on display with the Avro Lancaster now occupying the pride of place in the Aeroplane Hall. The fact that the AWM had to rely on the RAAF and volunteers to undertake restorations of the aircraft in their collection is a sad reflection of the times when the work was undertaken. Today the restoration team has trained conservators to oversee and document the restoration of any items in the AWM.

Endnotes:

1. The B. u type was most probably the Albatros D.I (D.391/16) of Ltn Büttner of *Jasta* Boelcke that was captured by the British intact, on 1 December 1916. It has Bü painted on the fuselage as Büttner's personal marking.
2. The quotes are from Gatherwood's Log Book. 'Soldier, Test Pilot, Dentist.' Manuscript in RAF Museum J.M. Bruce Collection Box 62.
3. The book has been republished several times since.
4. Lewis, C. *Farewell to Wings,* Temple Press Books, London, UK, 1964. P.63.
5. The report has a date stamp of 16 March 1918. Report on G.101. TNA AIR1/1193/204/5/2599.

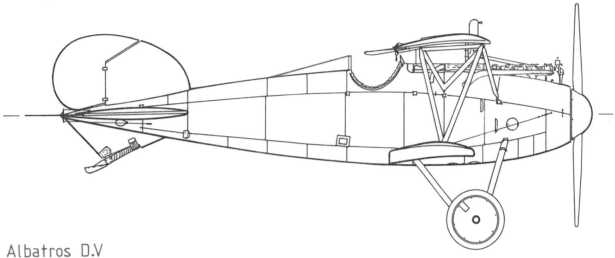

Albatros D.V
Note aileron cables pass into upper wing.

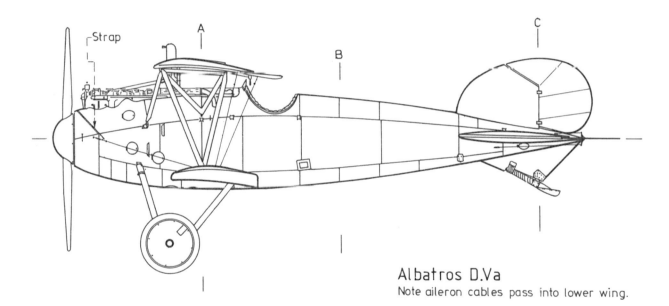

Albatros D.Va
Note aileron cables pass into lower wing.

Specifications Albatros D.Va:
Dimensions: Span 9.05 m; Length 7.33 m; Height 2.7 m
Wing Area: 21.2 m²
Weights: Empty 687 kg (including water); Loaded 937 kg
Performance: Speed 165 km/hr (max); Climb to 1,000 m 4
minutes Ceiling 5,700 m; Endurance 2 hrs.

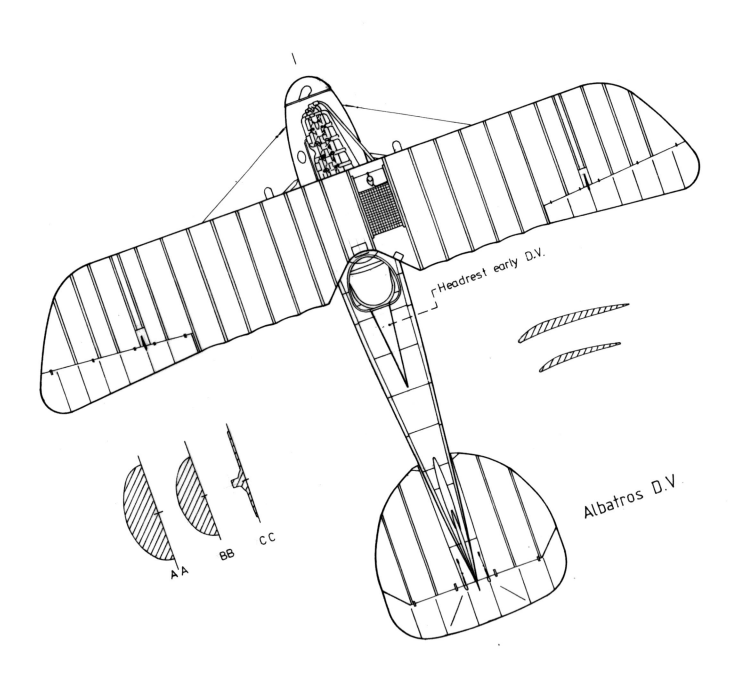

Headrest early D.V.

Albatros D.V

A A   B B   C C

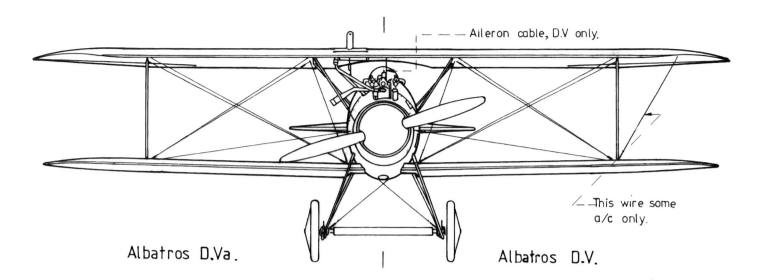

Aileron cable, D.V only.

This wire some a/c only.

Albatros D.Va.

Albatros D.V.

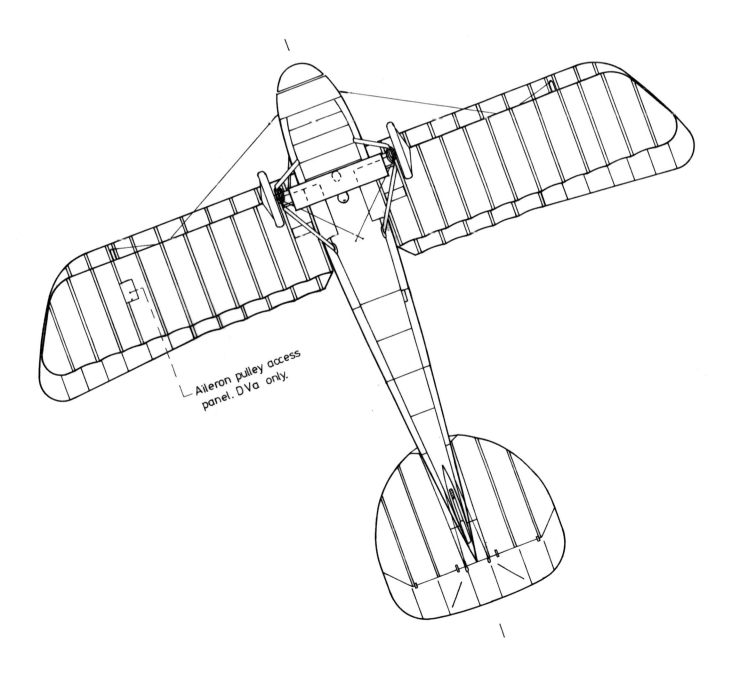

Aileron pulley access panel. DVa only.

Bibliography

Articles

'Dead Men in the sky!' *Australian Post*, July 27, 1967. P.2.

'Historic Canberra Visit.' *ASWWIAH Newsletter*. August 2008.

Dunnell, B. 'Living Memory.' *Aeroplane*, UK. September 2023. P.14.

Gröschel, D.H.M. 'Information on Ltn.d.Res. Clauss.' July 2001. Author's collection.

Lalas, H. 'The 1966 Restoration of Albatros D.Va' (as told by Harold and Alan Thomas in 1995). *Aviation Heritage*. June 2015. P.80.

Owers, C. 'Australia's First Museum.' *Air Enthusiast* No.47, Key Publishing, UK.

Parnell, N.M. 'An Albatros in Australia.' *Air Pictorial*. April 1968. P.125.

Pegram, Dr A. 'The Last Flight of the Albatros.' *The 14-18 Journal*. ASWWIAH 2022. P.20.

Watson, E. 'The Daimler Mercedes Aerofoil Radiator.' *The 14-18 Journal*. ASWWIAH.

Books:

Part Albatros D.V manual via R Waugh.

Bruce. J.M. *RAF RE8*. Datafile No. 24. Albatros Productions, UK. 1990.

Cutlack, F.M. *The Australian Flying Corps in the Western and Eastern Theatres of War 1914-1918*. Angus & Robertson Ltd, Australia. 1953.

Franks, N., Bailey, F. and Duiven, R. *The Jasta Pilots,* Grubb Street, UK, 1996.

Franks, N., Bailey, F. & Duiven, R. *The Jasta War Chronology*, Grub Street, UK, 1998.

Franks, N.; Bailey, F. & Duiven, R. *Casualties of the German Air Service 1914-1918*, Grub Street, UK. 1999.

Grosz, P.M; Haddow, G. & Schiemer, P. *Austro-Hungarian Army Aircraft of World War One,* Flying Machine Press, USA, 1993.

Hare, P.R. *RAF RE8 at War.* Datafile No. 153. Albatros Productions, UK. 2012. $50.

Herris, J. *Development of German Warplanes in WWI.* Aeronaut Books, USA, 2012.

Herris, J. *Albatros Aircraft of WWI Vol.4 – Fighters.* Aeronaut Books, USA. 2017.

Hobson, C. *Airmen Died in the Great War 1914-1918 – The Roll of Honour of the British and Commonwealth Air Services of the First World War,* JB Hayward & Son, UK, 1995

Mikesh, R.C. *Albatros D.Va German Fighter of World War I.* Smithsonian Institution Press, USA, 1980.

Nelmes, M. *A Unique Flight – The historic aircraft collection of the Australian War Memorial.* New Holland, Australia. 2008.

Owers, C.A. *Albatros D.V/D.Va at War, Vol.1,* Windsock Datafile No.151, Albatros Productions, UK, 2012

Rimell, R. *Albatros Fighters.* Windsock Datafile Special. Albatros Productions, UK. 1991.

Rogers, L. *British Aviation Squadron Markings of World War I RFC, RAF, RNAS,* Schiffer Publishing, USA, 2001.

Robertson, B. *British Military Aircraft Serials 1912-1969,* Ian Allen, UK, 1969.

Schaedel, C. *Albatros Scouts Described.* Kookaburra Technical Publications, Australia. No date.

Schiemer, P. *Die Albatros (Oeffag) Jagdflugzeuge der k.u.k. Luftfahrtruppen,* H weishaupt Verlag, Graz, 1984.

Wrigley, H.N. *The Battle Below. Australia.* No date. Limited edition reprint.

Files in the Australian War Memorial, the Australian and UK National Archives.

Made in United States
North Haven, CT
28 July 2024

55513319R00069